Tobias Rapp
Lost and Sound

Berlin, Techno and the Easyjet Set

Translated from the German by Paul Sabin

Published by Innervisions 2010 (www.innercityvisions.com)
All rights reserved
Original German version published by © Suhrkamp Verlag Frankfurt am Main 2009
All rights reserved

No part of this publication may be reproduced, stored in a retrieval system, or transmitted in any form or by any means, without the prior permission in writing of the publisher, nor be otherwise circulated in any form of binding or cover other than that in which it is published and without a similar condition including this condition beeing imposed on the subsequent purchase.

ISBN 978-3-942188-00-5

Proof-reading by Nicholas Grindell
Photography by Ali Ghandtschi (www.ghandtschi.de)
Art direction and design by Ta-Trung (www.ta-trung.com)
Project management by Steffen Berkhahn
Printed by H. Heenemann GmbH, Berlin (www.heenemann-druck.de)

INNERVISIONS
2010

Contents

- 08 Preface: Berlin, techno
- 20 The week begins: Wednesday
- 30 The birth of a club mile
- 70 So many languages here: Thursday
- 80 The Easyjet set and Europe's new clubbing geography
- 104 Berlin night life rests upon four pillars: Friday
- 116 Ricardo
- 128 Berghain, the centre of the world (by Alexis Waltz)
- 142 Queuing, going to Berghain, never wanting to go home: Saturday
- 158 The gentle bliss of the post-euphoric high: Sunday
- 170 72-hour party people: Bar 25
- 188 News from where the grass is greener
- 198 Berlin abroad
- 210 Partying until your hair starts to glow: Monday
- 216 Rave mother, rave daughter
- 232 The great techno assembly kit
- 248 We sell taste
- 260 Back to square one: Wednesday (reprise)
- 270 Twenty records: a brief history of the Berlin sound of the noughties
- 286 Thanks
- 287 Sources

Preface: Berlin, techno

This book was written to tell Berliners something about Berlin. That's how it started. Outside Germany, there's a common misconception that techno and house are so prevalent here that every bakery greets its customers with an early-morning dose of repetitive beats. That's not the case. Sure, the scene is extremely vibrant, but most of the time if you switch on the radio you'll hear the same rock and pop music as in other countries. Even the stations aimed at an urban audience play hip hop and R&B. Techno and house occupy a niche. A spacious niche, yes, but a niche all the same.

While I was working on this book, people with no direct knowledge of electronic music were often astonished when I outlined what it was about: 'Techno? Really? That's still around?' Even in Berlin, techno is thought of as the soundtrack to the Love Parade – a musical style which disappeared along with the nineties. Most Berliners know nothing of the secret life which attracts thousands of people to the clubs at night. That's what I wanted to talk about.

I started with three ideas. Firstly, there was the Berlin after-party scene which formed around the year 2003. It wasn't that it had a particularly groundbreaking sound; the music was firmly rooted in the minimal house and techno blueprints of previous years. What struck me as new was the way these parties functioned. Now, instead of being about having a 'night out'. the focus was on the next day. The second thing was that around this time a new 'club mile' was forming: the most influential Berlin clubs took up residence along the banks of the Spree. And thirdly, you began to hear more and more foreign languages in the queues for the clubs: the Easyjet set had landed in Berlin. The book was published in summer 2008.

For 'Lost and Sound' to be published in English is a great honour for me, and it's largely down to the fact that it ultimately became a book about more than just Berlin. Although Berlin is in the title and the majority of what's described takes place in Berlin, this is also a book about Europe. The countries of this continent are growing closer together, and their populations are just beginning to find narratives for the new entity which is emerging. We're seeing the formation of new public networks which aren't bound by national frameworks, and the way people are adopting them so naturally is quite remarkable when you consider how novel and extraordinary it actually is to be able to communicate without any consideration for national boundaries.

The international dimension of the Berlin music scene might be taken for granted by people who live in London, Paris or New York. But not by Berliners. Berlin has no financial industry, no media industry; not a single one of the blue-chip companies from Germany's DAX index has its headquarters in Berlin; there's no port here; Berlin just has politics and culture – and yet it has three and a half million residents. It's like a spaceship which has come to rest on the sandy Brandenburg soil, a curious metropolis made up of several little towns and with no real centre.

This means that the extraordinary development which electronic music has seen in Berlin in recent years is inextricably tied to the specific conditions present in this city: without its economic decline, its low cost of living, its liberal authorities and its experienced party promoters who learned their trade in the post-reunification chaos of the nineties, this development wouldn't have been possible.

Nevertheless, when you're standing in the queue for a club you get the distinct impression that this golden age of Berlin clubbing is the result of an international dynamic, not a local one, that these energies which culminate in Berlin largely emanate from other parts of the world, and particularly from people who've come here from the USA or from Northern and Southern Europe. Some have just come for a weekend in Berlin, some for a couple of months or longer. Aside from the diplomatic corps, the techno and club scene must surely be Berlin's most international domain. Of course, this is basically an instance of labour migration: clubbing is for Berlin what the financial industry is for New York or London, what Hollywood is for Los Angeles and what fashion is for Paris or Milan.

The way the German mainstream ignores club culture forms a stark contrast to the illusions held by many artists who flock to Berlin from all parts of the world. How often has it been claimed that the atmosphere in Berlin is reminiscent of Manhattan in the early eighties! The comparison is not so far-fetched – both then and now it was the artistic fertility of a city in economic and financial straits which radiated its appeal throughout the world and attracted hordes of creative individuals whose first priority was not climbing the global career ladder but expressing themselves and experimenting in a sheltered environment. The parallels end there, however, as the key element in New York at that time was the contact between Afro-American youths from the Bronx and Harlem and white artists from downtown. From there, hip hop prepared for its big break and went on to become the most successful pop culture of the last 25 years. The biggest pop star of recent decades also came out of the downtown scene: Madonna.

There's no Madonna on the horizon in Berlin. The only global star the Berlin scene has produced is the Canadian musician Peaches, and she's originally a phenomenon of the nineties, of what you might call Berlin-Mitte 1.0, an era oriented by different constellations to the Berlin of today.

So no, this Berlin of the noughties is actually different in many respects to the New York of the eighties. The biggest difference is probably that the stars of this city are not individuals but collective subjects: the Berlin clubs and their crowds. They're world famous, unique, and always ready to act as projection screens and take on new meaning. People travel from far and wide and wait patiently in queues to see these clubs for themselves, to celebrate them, and to become part of the party.

Berlin's exceptional status also has a historical tradition: since the sixties the city has been a particularly successful site of social experimentation. This is often overlooked, disputed or regarded as a weakness to be rectified in order to introduce to Berlin the same normality which applies in other cities – whatever this normality is held to be. In fact, the relative anonymity and facelessness of the Berlin techno scene are a great accomplishment which cannot be stressed enough – for even the accusations that someone or other has let the fame go to their head are essentially proof of the importance of staying firmly grounded. At a time when most of the stories told by a culture are focused solely on personalities, when an over-hyped celebrity cult reigns over all of society, it's good to know that at least one slice of culture has remained immune, where celebrity is seen for what it is: a waste of time.

No stars, then, and no sponsors either. Anyone who went clubbing in the nineties will remember how omnipresent the cigarette companies and mobile phone operators were back then in clubs all over Europe. Those times are gone too. Aside from the drinks company Red Bull, visible sponsors have withdrawn from the techno scene – in Germany at least – and no one misses them.

Seen through slightly rose-tinted spectacles, you could say that Berlin's house and techno scene has retained the positive elements of an independent culture – economic autonomy, artistic integrity, the refusal to compromise – whilst simply leaving the negative features – facile capitalist critique, idealisation of self-exploitation, a lack of professionalism – by the wayside. You could call it being independent without being indie: the ideal state of pop culture and the exact opposite of that rock and pop music which today is called indie, and which in most cases even sounds like indie, but which is very rarely independent.

In fact, there's another parallel with the American cities of the eighties which certainly applies to the Berlin techno scene. After the great record industry crash of 1979, disco music withdrew to the underground scene of the clubs and reinvented itself in new forms. The rhythms were mechanised, new styles and sounds were incorporated, and this development led a few years later to house, a genre which clearly follows in the tradition of disco and yet was also something completely new. It's a similar story with techno and Berlin in the noughties. The nineties were about rave and everything that went with it: great excitement, fantastic records, fantasies of world domination, chart entries; and then, after all the great successes and excesses, the whole thing collapsed as the end of the decade approached. Around the turn of the century the music went back underground in order to revitalise itself.

This book is about what happened next. It sheds light on the particular circumstances present in Berlin which allow so much to happen that would be unthinkable elsewhere. It speaks of wasteland, empty buildings and cheap rents, liberal authorities, tireless activists and techno institutions which simply keep on going. It discusses the importance of the scene for the politics of the city, and the liberalisation of the European air travel market which has allowed it all to grow to an undreamt of scale within such a short time. And it is about how the protagonists – DJs, producers, promoters, clubbers – live their scene, whether on a euphoric Saturday night or at an after-party on a Monday evening.

Along the way, **Lost and Sound** also tells a second, more personal story. I moved to Berlin in the summer of 1990 and have been going clubbing regularly ever since. There have been gaps. For a couple of years I only took a marginal interest in the city's nightlife. Nevertheless, I could tell a large portion of my life story by talking about the clubs where I spent my nights. Many friendships have been forged on these nights out, and some have even made it into the daylight.

The same will be true for many people who've been clubbing in Berlin in this period. Everyone has that place which, for them, is charged with the greatest truth. This is the place which counts, where the things that really matter get worked out, where you feel you are part of the world, where you have an ideal point of contact to other like-minded people and the spaces they inhabit. This place acts as a reference for everywhere else you like to spend your time. Previously it might have been the kitchen of a shared flat, or the street. For me and for many others I've met over the past twenty years in Berlin, this place is the club. The place where history is made, where you feel that what's happening here is part of one big Now.

Of course, seen in the cold light of day, this feeling is highly dubious and by and large nonsense. However, this does nothing to change the fact that it motivates thousands of people to go out raving night after night. Incidentally, it also has far less to do with politics than people believed at certain euphoric moments in the nineties.

Another aim of this book is to describe the conditions which come together to create moments of dance floor bliss. This feeling is transient and unpredictable. You may know what DJs you like and what music you're into, but it's impossible to say whether any particular night out has this special moment in store. It either happens or it doesn't. Often you'll stick around well into the next day just in case.

Some readers might be bothered by the term 'techno' in the subtitle of this book. Why not house? And they'd be right – for me personally and for most of the DJs and producers I spoke to in the course of my research, the umbrella term for electronic dance music is house. House music. In terms of music history, any number of reasons may be cited for this, but the popularity of the term 'house' seems to boil down to two things: firstly it refers to the place, the warehouse, where this music was first played. This makes house a more open concept than 'techno', a term which refers in a more abstract and intellectual way to a certain way of interacting with technology. Secondly, house has given rise to the historical subject known as the 'house nation': the people who dance to this music. This also remains an extremely attractive concept to this day.

In recent years a tendency has emerged in Germany to call this music 'electro'. I avoid this wherever possible, as electro has historically been a relatively discrete genre within electronic dance music. It has its roots in the breakdance music of the late seventies and early eighties and has basically never disappeared since. Electro thrives on retrofuturistic sounds, which means that it sounds like the music of the future as imagined in the eighties. It's full of simple computer game tones and early drum machine patterns. Another difference is that most electro music is driven by a broken 4/4 rhythm.

And what about minimal, or even mnml? Many critics like the term because it signals a departure from the beefed-up rave sounds of the nineties and clearly highlights the way the music of the noughties broke away from that of the previous decade. Unfortunately, the critics are the only ones who see it this way. Hardly anyone else actually uses the term.

In any case, whether it's techno, house, electro or minimal, anyone hoping to read a book primarily about music will probably be disappointed. Like any living pop culture, techno has an extremely short lifespan: a record stays big for a few weekends, sometimes for a whole season if it's extremely well received. Then it disappears, making room for new records. It might resurface after a couple of years because a certain element happens to sit nicely with the latest sound and DJs can dig it out of their crates to surprise a dance floor. But the public forum for these discussions is in the various magazines, on websites, and of course in the record shops and the clubs themselves. A book is too slow for this purpose.

This isn't a tourist guide either. There are no addresses listed at the back, no clubbing tips and no rules of etiquette. If you're looking for a club, you'll find it. If you can't, you should be trying a little harder.

It should also be noted that I only mention a few of the hundreds of DJs active in Berlin. Those whose names appear in this book are no more important than any others. If you leave aside for a moment certain extraordinary figures like Ricardo Villalobos, who plays a central role, then whichever way you look at this scene will involve a large slice of chance and personal preference. So this book is no encyclopaedia.

And it's no history book either. Although it became clear as I was researching that many people would like to see a history of the Berlin house and techno scene, the present alone appeared so rich that I wouldn't even know where to start with a history book. There's simply too much happening right now. This music and this special party culture associated with Berlin in the noughties is still so insistent on moving with the times that the task of penning history can happily be left for another day when there's less going on. The pop culture of yesterday isn't going anywhere – unlike that of today.

'Don't forget to go home,' the British DJ and producer Ewan Pearson – one of the many Anglophones from both sides of the Atlantic who have made it over to Berlin in recent years – warned the Berlin clubbing community three years ago in Maja Classen's documentary film **Feiern**. It's an illusion to think that happiness can be extended indefinitely. A few months later, writing a column in **Groove** magazine, Pearson back-pedalled: in view of the unique nature of many Berlin clubs, he said, and the danger that they may soon have to close, the primary duty of all ravers is to fight for their survival, to enjoy the beauty of these places, and to go out clubbing.

I have little to add to this. Reading this book is one thing; going clubbing is another. Lost in sound, lost and sound.

The week begins: Wednesday

It's not long after midnight, and if the city is sleeping at all, it's doing so elsewhere. The last U-Bahn is rumbling along the elevated steel track, about to cross the Oberbaumbrücke bridge into Friedrichshain. We're at Schlesisches Tor in Kreuzberg, Berlin. Not long ago this spot was anything but vibrant; the **Wrangelkiez,** a neighbourhood squashed in between Görlitzer Park, the Spree, the Landwehr canal and the traffic artery of Skalitzer Straße, was one of Kreuzberg's forgotten corners. This was still the case at the end of the nineties, when nightlife was centred around the Mitte district and techno was officially 'over'. Small groups of people are making their way along Falckensteinstraße towards the river bank. Two English visitors emerge somewhat puzzled from a courtyard and ask the way. 'Watergate?' – 'The door over there, up the stairs.' It's Wednesday, the weekend is still two working days away, and the butterflies are already there.

There's always something ceremonious about walking into a club. You go down the stairs, past the cigarette machine, towards the bar, and you look around. The first thing you check out as you enter a club is always the other people. Who's here? Who do I know? What's going on today? Watergate is right on the Spree, and the Waterfloor, the lower of the two levels, has a dance floor from which you can look out onto the river. You're perhaps two meters above the water level. The façade is fully glazed, from the floor to the ceiling. You look out at the river and the large building on the other bank where Universal Music Group has its German headquarters. A huge company logo, several storeys high, lights up in shifting colours. No ships pass by at night; the U-Bahn doesn't start running until a few hours later when the first workers have to commute; the brick arches of the bridge block the view of any motorists almost entirely. The logo is lit up just for those dancing in Watergate. For us.

Slowly the club gets busier, and around one o'clock there's this magic moment when the dance floor fills up. It happens quite quickly, and no one knows exactly how. It's as if someone pulled a lever. First there are just three people dancing, a few minutes later it's a couple of dozen. Then there are cheers. What's going on here? Is it the group of English clubbers that just arrived? Is it a particular track? Or a particular sound in a track, the house piano perhaps? In any case, the dance floor is full, and it will stay that way until the first computers are powered up at Universal.

'My My & Friends' is the name of the night. The promoters are the DJ and production duo My My: Nick Höppner and Lee Jones. Höppner comes from Hamburg, has been DJing for many years, and spent some time as an editor of **Groove**, an electronic dance music magazine. Now he works for Ostgut Ton, the label of the famous Berghain – but that club is closed on Wednesdays. 2006 saw the release of My My's debut album **Songs Of The Gentle**. Since then Höppner has been booked to play all over the world.

Lee Jones is from England; he came to Berlin at the start of the noughties. At the time he was more into the downtempo and broken beats scene. He brought out a few records under the alias Hefner. In Berlin he immersed himself in the minimal house scene, went clubbing more and more often, began playing live, and more recently began DJing as well. Today he's presenting his solo album **Electronic Frank.** It's being released on Aus Records, a British label managed by the DJ Will Saul. He's here too.

There are several clubs which have similar arrangements for midweek nights as Watergate has with Jones and Höppner. A night is allocated to a DJ team or a small label, thus allowing the club to make increased use of its capacity. After all, the rent has to be paid for Wednesdays and Thursdays too, whether there is an event on or not. The DJs, for their part, have a constant source of income based on how successful their night is. Essentially, it's a win-win situation. Not only is the club using its capacity, it's also cultivating its reputation without taking any risks. The DJs get a platform which allows them to invite fellow artists to play, and they may receive a return invitation.

Few DJs view their occupation purely in business terms. It's always about the party, having fun, the pleasure of playing the records they really want to play, and testing people's reactions to new music. What they're making into a career is not just their hobby, but their nocturnal lives as a whole. Those who have a regular slot can develop their style, try things out, work on their skills. Touring the world is one thing – glamorous and wonderful. A residency in your home city is another – it allows you to grow.

'My My & Friends' takes place once a month. Only the Waterfloor is open, but the night consistently gets two to three hundred guests through the doors. Who are these people who apparently don't have to get up for work the next day? What does it consist of, this social subject which is most often referred to simply as 'the scene', for want of another term?

One instantly recognisable fact is that a whole host of musicians and DJs are in attendance. Wednesday is a day when there's not too much else going on, when artists are generally not booked for appearances outside of the city, so they are free to go out just for pleasure. A few of the DJs have a small entourage with them: their girlfriends, booking agents or label bosses.

They are joined by guests from elsewhere, people lured to the city and this club by Berlin's reputation as a clubbing capital. The Japanese couple, for instance, who later get an autograph from the DJ. Or a group of Italians who look like an agency out on a work trip: two men and a lady in their mid fifties, three men of around thirty, and two women of around twenty. They're loving every minute. There are also the clubbing scene tourists, mostly from England, Scandinavia and Spain, who, at a glance, are no different to the locals. They dress similarly and have similar cultural preferences to the students and freelancers who live in Berlin, although most of these people aren't from here either.

Then in among these groups are a few real Berliners. It's not that you'd recognise them by their clothes, rather by their topics of conversation. Two guys on unemployment benefit joke that they're the only ones in the place who have to seriously worry about the next morning – everyone else's parents will foot the bill. But essentially they're doing fine, otherwise they wouldn't be merrily dancing away in here. One of them is an artist, the other keeps his head above water by doing cash-in-hand jobs. The artist has an important appointment early the next afternoon which he mustn't miss, some kind of seminar for people setting up their own businesses.

We stand at the bar and talk about how things used to be. Was it different? Better? Can euphoria stay with you as you grow older? What happened to drum'n'bass anyway? We talk about Goa raves, get onto the Middle East conflict, and from there to New York, where the artist and I have both lived for a while, that bizarre city which has decided that, for all its riches, it can't afford a nightlife. Now it basks in the light of its legendary past, gorged and lazy to the point of losing its appetite for contemporary pop culture. And we talk about how New Yorkers are always searching for New York, even when they go somewhere else, like Berlin. In Berlin it's most likely the New York of the eighties that they're looking for. Or is it the Berlin of the twenties? We talk our way around the world in eight minutes.

Clubbing conversations do have a tendency to revolve mainly around clubbing itself: how brilliant everything is again at the moment and whether to head over to that new club you've heard about from your mate who met that guy there. Or you have the opposite conversation: how you've really been getting the feeling lately that you can't go on like this. That after all this partying you really would like to focus more on your work, your studies, your relationship. Or your parents, who are getting old. That taking a break is actually really good. During this conversation you look around, see that girl you were introduced to earlier, and think: okay, don't forget her name.

Watergate also has another larger room, one which produces genuinely glamorous moments with the help of its giant strip of LED lights. As you dance underneath it, you have the impression of having stepped into an R&B music video. Although this room is only open at weekends, we go up. Someone has a key. Surprisingly there's something going on here too. There's no crowd, but a couple of people who normally work at Watergate have met up to play records over the big sound system and switch on the lights. 'Well,' says one of them, 'one thing better than listening to music is listening to music loud.'

Then we head back downstairs. It's half past three and the action has shifted almost completely to the dance floor. Just a couple of people are still standing at the bar; the space in front of the DJ booth is full. People dance together, communicate in little clusters, bring each other beer, water and spirits, urge on the DJ and cheer when he takes out the bass only to slam it back in a few beats later.

There's a pleasant casualness, but also something extreme, about going out on a Wednesday, not least due to the charm of participating in a parallel society. Basically, a space is created here which brings together two fairly distinct groups which you wouldn't immediately put together in your mind: the DJs and the clubbing tourists. It's not as if the locals have left yesterday's tired clubs to the tourists and moved on to newer and cooler locations. Quite the opposite: the night gains its vitality from the combination of DJs feeling they can experiment freely and clubbing tourists (who, incidentally, know exactly which clubs are hip right now, as these days nothing is too underground to appear on the internet) who dance as if there were no tomorrow. After all, that's the main reason they came to the city. To the place where, on a Wednesday, in an intimate atmosphere, they can see the same artists who might appear just once in a month of party Saturdays in their home city. It's a situation with considerable potential – the DJs get the clubbers revved up, and vice versa.

Of course, this also results in some more bemusing moments as the night wears on. At some point someone enlightens me on the concept of 'hedge fund house'. The brilliant thing about DJ sets, he says, is that even if you don't like certain tracks, the sets can still be enjoyed as a whole. This is like hedging your bets, he says: You can't lose. Stands to reason.

Later the Japanese girl who earlier asked for an autograph is standing at the edge of the dance floor with her jacket on, her bag on her shoulder, waiting for her boyfriend to finally prise himself away from the action. They have several discussions, but neither of them appears to lose patience. In the small adjoining room behind the toilets, visible from the DJ booth through a glazed wall, couples lounge and smooch on the sofas.

Then dawn begins to break. There's not a cloud in the sky; slowly its dark inky hue grows lighter, and if you look eastwards down the Spree you can see the rosy-fingered dawn turning by degrees into that yellowish beige, the one which could be caused by the local factory emissions, or by the sand carried in the air around here, you never quite know. 'Hey, look at that,' I say to the guy next to me and point outside. 'What?' he says. 'The sky, yeah, seen it before.'

Time to go. Plans are made to meet up at the weekend. The week has only just begun.

The birth of a club mile

A five-kilometre stretch between Alexanderplatz and the Oberbaumbrücke bridge is now home to most of the city's clubs. The no-man's land along the banks of the Spree exhibits an overlapping of investors' dreams and political intentions, urban planning and left-wing activism, through-traffic and raver's paradise.

A city is there to be interpreted. It does not divulge the meaning of its symbols to everyone. You have to know how to decipher them. A new clubbing district has evolved in central Berlin, a club mile which attracts many thousands of people every weekend and which has long-since gained a worldwide reputation. And yet, for the uninitiated, it remains virtually invisible: a secret, hidden world, right in the centre of the capital.

How many of those driving to work on a sunny Monday morning would suppose that a few people dotted around the central embankment of a busy road linking Treptow and the city centre could have something to do with it? Or the innocuous flashes of colour you see at night driving northwards alongside Alexanderplatz if you look up at a tower block while waiting at the lights? Or the small groups emerging on a Sunday afternoon from an industrial estate behind the old prefab office building where the newspaper **Neues Deutschland** has its headquarters? You can pass through Berlin's new club mile without even noticing it. You can ride all the way through it on your bike in about a quarter of an hour and see nothing more than a few building sites. This is certainly true in the daytime, but also to an extent at night. Only the occasional massing of taxis tells you there's a party going on around here somewhere.

The northern end of the club mile is marked at Alexanderplatz by Weekend, a club located in 'Haus des Reisens', an old GDR tower block, occupying three of its upper floors. There's a gaping hole in the street in front of the building ('Building work until 2011', says a sign). On the other side a new shopping centre is being built – the only implemented project from a so-called master plan for the area which was conceived in the mid-nineties, and to which the tower block which accommodates Weekend is also expected to fall victim at some point. That's the theory, anyway. First, investors must be found for a new tower block, and that could take some time.

Less than a kilometre further south, in a bend in the S-Bahn tracks by Jannowitzbrücke station, is the door to Golden Gate, concealed among the graffiti covering the walls. The entrance to Sage Club, a few hundred metres along in the same direction, still looks just like it used to when it was called Boogaloo or Walfisch: an inconspicuous door in an U-Bahn station. If you turn left here, from Heinrich-Heine-Straße into Köpenicker Straße, then you're a stone's throw from the new Tresor. Apart from a sign on the entrance, you can only identify the club from the street at night, when a spotlight projects the enormous club logo onto the façade of the former power plant. During the day it's almost invisible. A little further down the road on the opposite side is Relais. Across the Spree, on Holzmarktstraße, is Bar 25, famed throughout the world, but invisible for Berliners who aren't in the know. All you can see from the street is some pale fencing with a gate. Then a couple more minutes walk away there's Maria, on Schillingbrücke, which looks like part of the backdrop to a nineties theme park: a rugged shack on the banks of the Spree.

Over the road and to the right is Ostbahnhof station. If you head half a kilometre northwest from here you reach an industrial semi-wasteland where, between building sites, car parks, a field and a small stream, lies Berghain, a club located in an old power plant from the fifties which was never hooked up to the grid. A majestic concrete castle. If you return to the river from here, then head a little further away from the city centre and switch to the other bank again, then Watergate is on your left. It's situated by the Oberbaumbrücke which spans the river between Friedrichshain and Kreuzberg, and it looks like it has found its way onto the outermost tip of this district in order to attach itself as closely as possible to the uninhabited area which runs a couple of kilometres through the city on the east side of the Spree. Just around the corner from here is Club der Visionäre, and that concludes this walk through three city districts – from Alexanderplatz to Schlesisches Tor, or to Treptower Park if you also include Arena Club, Badeschiff, and the grassland area Schlesischer Busch, where you can have a lie down between two after-parties on a summer afternoon. You can stroll it in three quarters of an hour. The whole stretch is made up of two large streets which form a corridor. This is where the ravers are to be found, for days and nights on end.

No one likes the term club mile; it sounds like the focal point of an 18-30s holiday. Like Simon-Dach-Straße in Friedrichshain or Oranienburger Straße in Mitte, where the bars are lined up side by side and huge groups of tourists are herded between them on the epic binges they call pub crawls. These are streets which, in a few years, have evolved from trendy meeting spots into areas where most people you meet are strangers to the city. Where even the majority of the bar staff only carry on working there because the money flowing into the tills night after night is adequate compensation.

This is not what the new Berlin club mile is about – even though it also attracts huge numbers of tourists who, it may be assumed, provide a decent nightly income for the clubs. Nevertheless, it has nothing to do with the strips of bars in other parts of the city. Firstly, it's too spread out, and secondly, this is about clubs. They open late, rarely before midnight; they charge an entry fee; they have bouncers; and their visitors normally come specifically because of the name of a DJ on the line-up or the reputation of the club. Even when they've come from far away, most of them have a fairly precise idea of where they want to go.

To Berghain, for instance, currently the most famous techno club in the world. Here, clubbers indulge in excess and explore constantly changing interpretations of techno music with an almost religious earnestness. Or to Bar 25, the equally legendary counterpart to the monumental Berghain. It's smaller, sunnier and more playful, an after-party location directly on the banks of the Spree where the parties often go on until Tuesday morning. Most of the clubs are located in the area where Friedrichshain and Kreuzberg, that odd pair of inner-city underdog districts, border one another. These two parts of the city are separated by several major roads, a few train lines, the Spree, and of course forty years of the Berlin Wall. They are connected by a strong feeling of regional identity and some miserable social statistics. The borough reform of the nineties merged them into a single administrative unit.

Club miles & more

The new Berlin club mile has a predecessor. Once before, the clubbing scene was concentrated in a single area, on a kilometre stretch of Leipziger Straße between Potsdamer Platz – which was still wasteland at the time – and Friedrichstraße. In the early nineties you would see more people here at night time, around clubs such as Tresor, E-Werk, WMF and others, than you would during the day. It was an urban no-man's land which was soon to be developed by investors, and one where a formidable pop-cultural dynamic developed for a period of a few years. Yes, techno was played elsewhere in the city at this time, but had it not been for this collection of small and large clubs in close proximity to one another, the friendships and hostilities, rivalries and alliances which accompanied it, and of course the excesses which were played out here, then techno would probably never have evolved into the dominant sound which inhabited the charts for a certain time, and which drew hundreds of thousands of ravers to the city for the Love Parade. It was a system of pop culture which gave rise to the term Raving Society, and which disappeared just as quickly as it had emerged.

There are certainly more parallels with the present time, in the music for example: the sound of the new Berlin club mile is firmly rooted in techno. Its chances of having comparable mainstream success can't be discounted, but the record industry has collapsed anyway, so how could current success be measured in comparison to back then? Certainly, if you look at the numbers of people dancing to this music every weekend, it has long-since reached the same appeal it had in the early nineties.

There are also other resemblances linking the area between Holzmarktstraße and Köpenicker Straße and this former club mile. Much of the area where the clubs are so densely packed today is also urban wasteland. This is not due to be the case for long, which is another parallel. Investors have already begun constructing the so-called MediaSpree, a new city district with offices for media firms. Unlike back then, however, there is currently fierce resistance to these plans. In the summer of 2008, the residents of Kreuzberg and Friedrichshain voted in a referendum that the development plans should be retracted.

The clubs back then were temporary; everyone knew that the magic could suddenly be over. As such, any refurbishments made to the clubs were provisional. You always ran the risk of having some ceiling plaster trickle into your gin and tonic when a certain bass frequency shook the room. This is not the case today. Not all the people who run the clubs in the area have long-term leases, but many do, and large sums have been invested: lights, sound, furnishings – once you set foot inside most of these clubs, there's nothing to remind you of the raw charm of the nineties.

Berlin is being reinvented here. It's not the West Berlin of the seventies, that battleground for alternative culture whose signature can be found on the rock records of Ton Steine Scherben and in the comics of Gerhard Seyfried. It's not the West Berlin of the eighties made famous by anarchist squatters, Mayday riots and the experimental band Einstürzende Neubauten, that peculiar village in the shadow of the wall described by Sven Regener in his **Herr Lehmann** trilogy. And it's not the East Berlin of the nineties, that adventure playground which turned the city into the backdrop for the Love Parade with its flamboyant dancers on walls, their faces still bearing the burden of history. This is certainly not the Berlin of the Aggro rappers, that cut-throat city where it's every man for himself and where crime lurks around every street corner. Nor does it have anything to do with those neo-Wilhelminian fantasies which surface time and again when politicians get on their soapboxes.

This new Berlin, which attracts thousands of clubbing tourists every weekend, is the party capital of the Western world. It's a city where the rents are cheap and the authorities are extremely liberal; where the reality principle of other cities is abandoned in favour of an all-embracing pleasure principle. No one really has to work here, except on some art or music project or other. There are constantly new clubs opening, and everyone just spends their time partying. That's top of the list.

Whether it's Berghain or Bar 25, Tresor or Watergate, the clubs of the new party district have made Berlin into a pop-cultural destination of choice; a city which successfully gives a great number of people the feeling that there are still places which have not sacrificed freedom for security – that there is another way.

This club doesn't need a sign

When Steffen Hack, or Stoffel, as everyone calls him, opened Watergate in autumn 2002, it was the only club in the area. Watergate is situated right by the Oberbaumbrücke, on the Kreuzberg side, a part of the district which used to be dead at night time. That wasn't the only special thing about the club. The decision to open it in a modern office building was also a statement: enough of converting old buildings; this is the start of something new. At least, that's the impression it made at the time. For the whole of the nineties, the misappropriation of old buildings had been one the most visible features of Berlin club culture. That's reading too much into it, says Stoffel now. He was simply happy to have found this place.

Stoffel is in his mid-forties and, having been in the city since 1982, a veteran of Berlin night life. He managed Toaster, a jungle and drum'n'bass club in Mitte, in the basement of the building where the Goethe Institute now has its headquarters. This gave rise to the series of 'hard:edged' parties which wandered from one location to another, not shying away from using premises illegally. This was nothing unusual in the nineties, but the dimensions it sometimes reached with the hard:edged parties was. There was a memorable drum'n'bass rave in what used to be a club called Planet, a run-down building on the banks of the Spree, behind what is now the German Architecture Centre. Without the faintest pretence of legality, Stoffel and his companions managed to get not only two large sound systems onto the site for its two dance floors, but also a huge aluminium rig from which a dozen monitors were hung – this was the great age of the video artists. Looking out across the river from Watergate, the site is located a few hundred metres downstream. Today it's just as deserted as it was back then, but more effectively sealed off. Numerous graffiti bear witness to the parties that were held there.

At some point, Stoffel grew tired of changing locations and organised a drum'n'bass night at WMF, a club which has moved around a few times itself. And then there was Watergate, a beautiful club by the water, with two rooms on separate floors and a terrace out on the water. We meet to talk in the so-called Waterfloor, a room with a fully glazed façade facing out onto the water with a beautiful view of the Spree and of the headquarters of Universal Music. At night time a giant company logo lights up on the Universal façade. Now, in the daytime, the building is just a hulking yellow mass on the opposite river bank.

Interestingly, and this is clearer in the daytime than at night, nothing on Watergate's door indicates that it's a club: no emblem, no sign. This is a deliberate omission, says Stoffel. He doesn't want to attract passing custom; he wants a clued-up crowd. Indeed, Watergate is one of Berlin's best-known clubs on the international stage, above all for its programme of minimal techno. This is despite the fact that Stoffel didn't actually want to have techno played in Watergate at first, and certainly not as its main focus. He had something else in mind, a club which followed the British pattern of drum'n'bass, breaks or hip hop on a Friday and house on a Saturday.

It soon became clear, however, that the plan wasn't working out as he'd expected. Especially since now around seventy percent of visitors to the club are from outside Berlin. 'Our guests come from all over the place, and they don't come here hoping to be surprised,' says Stoffel. 'If you don't put on pretty much the same thing every night, you confuse people and it doesn't work. It's sad, too, that people want so little diversity. But they want to be able to head back to Birmingham and say, "It's so awesome in Watergate." And then if they come back a couple of months later, they don't want to end up at a drum'n'bass night. Since we've been putting on house, techno or minimal every night, the club has been buzzing.' This also has a positive side, says Stoffel: 'At some point we realised that putting on techno and house not only allows you to make the most money, it also attracts the most intelligent, likeable and up-for-it crowd. And anyway, you don't run a club like this for the money.'

Nevertheless, without money, the whole operation isn't possible. Several hundred thousand euros have been invested in Watergate. The club has already been renovated twice, most recently in 2006 in order to install a giant LED lighting system on the upper floor. A third renovation is also on the horizon. The borough authorities are planning to have a promenade running along the river as part of the redevelopment of the banks of the Spree. Wherever the buildings go right out to the edge of the river a boardwalk is to be constructed for pedestrians. For Watergate, this means that the Waterfloor will have to be redesigned in the not-too-distant future. Much as everyone enjoys looking out onto the water while they dance, not many clubbers wish to be stared at by passers-by, and certainly not at six o'clock in the morning. Besides, the promenade will also get in the way of Watergate's terrace. So he'll have the floor at water level converted into a restaurant, says Stoffel, and the dance floor will move to a higher storey.

This brings us to the heart of the debate surrounding MediaSpree, the large-scale project to redevelop the land between the bridges Jannowitzbrücke and Elsenbrücke, an area of around 180 hectares along both banks of the Spree. Watergate is situated almost exactly in the geographical centre of this project. Most clubs on Berlin's new club mile are located either within or on the fringes of this development zone. Since the fall of the wall the clubs have always played a part in the big debate over the development of the city, in the nineties just as today.

Stoffel can air his grievances about the plans for the area at great length, starting with the fact that he is not allowed to place umbrellas with advertising logos or chains of lights on his terrace because it's directly in front of the Oberbaumbrücke, a listed monument. On the other side of the river, however, the operators of O2 World were given permission to erect an illuminated screen which lights up the whole area at night. Equally irksome for Stoffel is the fact that the people behind the MediaSpree project had the cheek to use pictures from Watergate in their advertising brochures, while in reality, he says, they don't take culture into consideration at all and are prepared to sacrifice anything to make a profit.

'After the collapse of East Germany, we in Berlin could have used the opportunity to plan a genuinely new city, a model city,' says Stoffel. 'There was so much wasteland, so much free space. It would have been possible to implement genuinely new urban development ideas. And what do we do with Potsdamer Platz? We copy the construction plans of other cities, let dim-witted investors cobble something together which they can sell on again in ten years. You can see the amount of interest there used to be in this site. And now MediaSpree, or as the investors say, the

Spreeraum. What's going on? Exactly the same thing. Why don't we have the courage, for once, to say, "Let's combine old and new. Let's have culture and investment." In hindsight the investors will actually be happy if they don't just end up with an area full of grey concrete towers.'

Swimming in the MediaSpree

The plans for MediaSpree, the petition for a referendum against the project and the consequences of that campaign make a remarkable story. It involves an association called MediaSpree e. V. which was founded in 2001 in order to bring together the landowners, investors and association representatives who had acquired plots of land in this huge area since the fall of the wall. As early as 1998 the 'Treptowers', a large complex of offices, were constructed on the West side of the Spree at the lower end of the area in question. In 2002, Universal Music moved into a former egg refrigeration warehouse diagonally opposite the towers, and two years later the TV station MTV took up residence in the building next door to Universal. It was also around this time that the run-down buildings on Mühlenstraße started being torn down. For several years these had been the home of the techno club Ostgut, the nucleus which expanded into Berlin's current techno scene. Casino, another club, was also located here. On the site of what used to be Ostgut now stands O2 World, a huge multi-purpose arena with capacity for 17,000 spectators. The ice hockey team Eisbären Berlin play there. They left their former home arena, the 'Corrugated Iron Palace' in Hohenschönhausen, for O2 World. Those fluent in the famous

Berliner Schnauze dialect have a fondness for naming local landmarks according to their apparent resemblances, hence 'pregnant oyster' for the congress hall, 'washing machine' for the chancellery, and now 'the drunken constable' for O2 World – the arena looks like an upside-down police cap.

Things were set to continue in this vein. The borough and the investors had lofty plans, including building offices on an area of several hundred thousand square metres, creating forty thousand jobs in the media industry, and rebuilding the Brommybrücke, a bridge destroyed during World War II. A narrow strip on the river bank was to remain accessible to pedestrians. Meanwhile, although the MediaSpree brochures have used pictures from local clubs to advertise the vibrancy of the area, neither Maria, nor Bar 25, nor any other local club with a temporary use contract appeared in the plans. That's just the way these things go. Or so we thought – and then came the petition for a referendum.

Petitions for a referendum have been permitted by the Berlin constitution as a tool of direct democracy since 2005. To date, 'Sink MediaSpree' has been the petition with the highest level of participation. The 16,000 signatures required in order to force a referendum were collected in record time, and the subsequent vote left no room for doubt: on 13 July 2008, 86.8% of Friedrichshain-Kreuzberg residents voted against the construction project and in favour of the alternative suggestion from the residents' initiative. With a turnout of 19.1%, this amounted to 34,932 ballots cast, out of the roughly 180,000 entitled to vote. Although the referendum doesn't have a binding effect, it will not go unheeded. The borough's first reaction was to appoint a special committee, which includes representatives of the residents' initiative, of the landowners, and of the borough itself, to examine the development options for each individual piece of land. It's a promising process, not least because many plots of land are owned by companies belonging to the state of Berlin. Just how long places like Yaam, Oststrand or Bar 25 will be able to remain here, however, is anyone's guess.

At the heart of the scene

One of those guessing is Christoph Klenzendorf. He's one of the four people behind Bar 25, situated in the centre of the new Berlin club mile, half way between Watergate and Weekend, between Berghain and Tresor, just beyond the Michaelbrücke. You can hardly see the entrance as you drive past; it's just a door in some pale fencing. Bar 25 is loved and hated, feared and revered, world-famous and yet relatively hidden. It plays a central role in the dispute over the future development of the area around the Spree, and not just because of its geographical location. The plot of land where it's situated belongs to the Berlin sanitation department. This is a municipal company, which means that it has a duty to take public considerations into account in its decisions. That's the theory, anyway. In practice, the relationship between Bar 25 and its landlord is anything but friendly. On 1 January 2008 the lease was terminated, and since the Bar 25 crew didn't accept the termination, in April they were served with an eviction notice. For the entire year, however, Klenzendorf and his companions simply acted as if nothing was wrong and carried on partying regardless. It was a bold move which eventually paid off for the Bar 25 crew, as the hearing before the Berlin District Court in December 2008 ended in a settlement. Although they were meant to have vacated the site long ago, they were able to come to an agreement with the sanitation department: they are allowed stay in operation until the end of August 2009. Then they must hand over the site 'broom clean' – they even have to saw down the trees which have grown there over the past five years.

Christoph Klenzendorf is a charismatic character. When he looks you in the eye and says, 'It's about partying,' you're prepared to follow his argument a long way. He's in his early thirties and very, very good looking, if you're into that slightly scruffy Berlin style or, as a friend of mine once said: he can make anything look stylish, even the old frilly dress he sometimes goes around in. Klenzendorf is living proof that excessive partying keeps you young and beautiful. If Bar 25 were a band, he would be the front man.

But it's not. Bar 25 is a commune of around fifteen people who live on the site and, with the help of around fifty employees, offer a range of services for leisure and pleasure: a spa, a restaurant in the upper price bracket, a hostel, a cinema, and in their 'spare time' they run a record label and a radio station. All these things are managed at once, and all to spectacular effect. Then of course, at the heart of it all, is 'the Bar' – an after-party location unparalleled in the western world. During the summer season its line-ups go right the way through from Friday evening to Monday afternoon. Every weekend. The promoters like to join in the party themselves; they even live on the site, in trailers parked behind the fence and in a couple of cabins which have been built in a small wooded area. The summer of 2008 was Bar 25's fifth season so far.

'No one knows what's in store for this area,' says Klenzendorf. 'We don't know, the city doesn't know, and nor do the investors. On one hand, it's clear to everyone that this space isn't needed for offices. On the other hand, there are also people who want to rake in as much cash for their borough as possible during their legislative period. Others say that we need a new concept, the old one has become out-dated, the development plans are wrong, Berlin has not turned out as people imagined it would, it has remained what it always was, a capital of culture. A city for creatures of leisure and free spirits. These development plans are destroying a lot of the spaces which, for many people, are places to live their lives and express themselves. This is what we are fighting against.'

Up to this point, the majority of Kreuzberg and Friedrichshain residents would probably agree with Klenzendorf – ultimately, when someone's singing the blues of the continual erosion of free spaces, anyone with their heart in the right place will join in. It's not quite that simple, however, and Klenzendorf knows this. 'A poster from the "Sink MediaSpree" campaign was once put up outside,' he says with a smile. 'It said "Spree banks for everyone". So I wrote underneath, "from Tuesday to Saturday".' Naturally, he says, 'Spree banks for everyone' is not his motto. 'We don't offer a space for everyone. We just offer a space for those who we want here.' And this is where the contradictions between Bar 25 and the larger consensus of borough residents begin: yes, that lot up there shouldn't be allowed to do whatever they want. But what about this lot down here?

In order to maintain their own parallel world, this lot down here have a fence in front of their site and a doorwoman whose nickname is, without a hint of irony, 'Door Hitler'. Such are the lives of the people who live and party here, they require secure barriers to separate them from the rest of the city. The excess and the hedonism to which people abandon themselves here at the weekend are not meant for the eyes of the public. The world out there wouldn't like what it saw.

For, ultimately, the parties are not organised in pursuit of a political goal. They are open to a political interpretation; everyone has their own political opinion, but no common political ground can be inferred from the fact that people are dancing together. Unless, of course, there is a threat of the dance floor being taken away.

MediaSpree opens up two political questions which often overlap. When it's a matter of the privatisation of public space, there's a resounding consensus among those opposed: no, we don't want it. Even if we are promised that jobs will be created. Even if we are warned that the borough will have to pay several million euros in contractual penalties if it backs out. However, there is also a second question which is not only more difficult to answer, but also more difficult to formulate. An initial attempt might be: how do we deal with alternative ways of living? The question has often been discussed in the past in Kreuzberg, Germany's best-known alternative district. If Bar 25 were just an unauthorized trailer park, its residents would have been cleared off the premises long ago – with or without a substitute location. But it's not as simple as that. Those behind Bar 25 are trailer park people, but they are also a group of investors, and for good measure they are also creators of culture – subculture even, which, in view of its radical insistence on self-determination, could certainly be classified as left-wing. The only catch is that not everyone is allowed to participate. It's a complex situation.

This is nothing new, however. Most sub-cultural developments of the last fifty years felt a greater commitment to the military logic of the avant-garde than to democratic participation: it was about being there first, exploring uncharted terrain, relaying information every now and again, but otherwise living the wild and dangerous life of small, secretive groups. Subcultures never want to be there for everyone, for in the mainstream lurks the danger of selling out. In the case of Berlin night life this has always taken the form of the two dreaded groups, **Touris** (tourists) and **Prolls** (proles). The emancipatory core of subcultures is always directed inwards. They study new forms of communal living, fight for a right to declare themselves independent from the big bad world.

This is how it is at Bar 25, too. 'We offer a space for the things we stand for,' says Klenzendorf, 'for this kind of culture, this way of life. For the people who want to live like this. They're perfectly welcome. I'm also fighting for the city, to have it remain as it is, to have Berlin continue to offer spaces for people who are different.'

Nevertheless, Klenzendorf (along with many others who live on the site) also has a clear sense of the transient nature of this situation – and of the beauty which this very nature affords. When asked which he is more afraid of – Bar 25 closing or Bar 25 not having to close, he says, 'Leave the party at its most beautiful moment. The place will never be able to remain as it is now. Everything's rotting here. It's a building site; it's not meant to be around forever. Even the substance of the site prevents it from functioning for very long. These concrete slabs have trees springing up between them. They'll soon fall down because they're not strong enough. The place is designed to last ten years, maybe fifteen. Just like our buildings; they're made of wood too, and they'll rot away. At some point it'll all be over. But it's also beautiful that it's so transitory; it means it will have been an experience for all those who were here. A fantastic time. A closed chapter. That's how it'll be, and I think that's great.'

It will have been a wonderful time. Perhaps the future perfect tense is the best way to describe the intense moments experienced at Bar 25, weekend after weekend. The Bar 25 crew have taken up the borough's invitation to participate in the special committee devoted to the future of the area – despite running the risk of playing a part in their own eviction.

Clubbing for the economy

'What makes Berlin stand out is its uncontrolled growth, the fact that not everything is properly structured. Without these free spaces, the whole industry wouldn't have emerged in the nineties. Of course, no one decided this back then either; there was no charity on the part of the establishment. The state authorities simply hadn't got that far yet, they didn't yet have a grip on the situation. That's why there were free spaces, and you could do things which weren't even conceivable elsewhere.' When Olaf Kretschmar talks about the nineties, you could be forgiven for thinking he means Bar 25.

Kretschmar, better known as Gemse, is the Chairman of the Berlin Club Commission, an association founded in the late nineties to represent the interests of Berlin's clubs, both to the various authorities and to the public. It has well over a hundred members.

Some of the larger clubs are missing, but the smaller ones are virtually all on board. The Club Commission is based in a small office near Alexanderplatz, half way between the Babylon cinema and the tower of the Berliner Zeitung newspaper offices. Gemse himself was an active club promoter in Berlin-Mitte in the nineties. The founding of the Club Commission was closely related to the collapse which the Berlin scene experienced in the late nineties. The chaos of the post-reunification period was over; a process of permanent professionalisation set in. The handy buzzword **Clubsterben** reared its head. Although in reality clubs weren't dying out altogether, it did sum up a situation which many had difficulty accepting at the time: those who wanted to survive would have to adapt. In the anarchic years after the fall of the wall the clubs had got by just fine on their own. Now they needed a lobby group. The commission's goal, as stated in its charter, is to work on 'maintaining favourable conditions for club culture'.

The idea was not free of controversy. After all, the speed at which a city's night life changes makes it the natural enemy of any meddling by associations. Today, however, the Club Commission enjoys recognition from all quarters. First and foremost because it does a good job. 'We're not simply a lobby group,' says Gemse. 'We offer training and we present the night life of the city to other associations, the Chamber of Industry and Commerce, and the music authors' society GEMA. We liaise with the senate, the borough authorities and industry players – basically with anyone who wants to have anything to do with the city's night life.' For example, the Club Commission played a role in negotiating Berlin's relatively liberal ruling on smoking areas when the smoking ban, or 'law to protect non-smokers', was introduced.

Above all, he never tires of singing the clubs' praises as sites of cultural production. 'Part of the music industry's value-creation chain', 'innovation', 'the social backstage of those places which are setting trends' – Gemse has precisely the persuasive tone you need for a radio panel discussion or a proposal document. For him, the clubs are part of the city's 'creative infrastructure'.

Today, Gemse says, the economic growth of a city is inseparable from the creative possibilities it offers. Now that the majority of industries have migrated away from Berlin, never to return again, the city can only survive by offering a good environment for creative people who – at this point he refers to modern industrial location theory – will draw businesses, and thus new jobs, to the city. Not the other way round. This is something that politicians have to react to, he says. Creatives, Gemse explains, like to be in a vibrant cultural environment, and this is not something which can be brought about by planning everything on a grand scale. This is why the authorities would be best advised to leave the clubs in peace. 'In this sector, planning means showing restraint. Of course there has to be a framework, construction guidelines, for example. But you have to give a city room to develop on its own.' A large step in the right direction would be to promote temporary use of spaces, for instance, or to exempt these short-lived clubs from the strict criteria for ventilation or toilets which apply to places with long-term leases.

Another point is that the clubs are now not only making their mark on the city, but also contributing to its upkeep. Clubbing has firmly established itself as an economic growth factor.

Quantifying the contribution of clubs to the local economy in precise terms is no easy task, however. The City of Berlin publishes a report on the music business every year, but the clubs are not treated as a separate category. In 2007, the turnover generated by concert promoters stood at 76 million euros, and that of concert venues was 140 million euros. No one knows what proportion the clubs contributed to these totals. Then there's a second study which the Club Commission has compiled on behalf of the city authorities. It's based on a survey of the Commission's members, conducted in 2005. According to the report, Berlin's clubbing industry employs around 8,000 people – roughly the same number working for Deutsche Telekom or Deutsche Post in the city. The members' turnover in 2005 added up to around 170 million euros, but this is likely to have increased significantly since then. Furthermore, these calculations only take the turnovers of the clubs themselves into account, not the total spending of the clubbing tourists on items such as accommodation, food, transport and shopping. Nor does it include the clubbing industry's effect on the image of the city and its appeal as a travel destination. The latter, in particular, appears to be considerable. According to a study by Berlin Tourismus Marketing GmbH, the clubs are now in second place behind the museums in a survey of tourists that asks which cultural institutions have drawn them to the city – well in front of the opera and theatre.

Interestingly, it's not the city's office of culture that's responsible for the clubs; they are allocated to the office for the economy. This is the department where Tanja Mühlhans works. She did the job of club representative for seven years before giving it up at the start of 2008 to switch her focus to the Berlin fashion scene.

Wherever we lay our hat

How might one imagine the job of Berlin's government representative for clubs? It was about two things mainly, says Tanja Mühlhans. Firstly, it was important to actually have a person to contact when, for instance, club promoters had problems with licenses or permits. The Berlin administration is structured on two levels: the city and its boroughs. When she started the job, the boroughs still treated clubs like bars and restaurants. The second aspect was about increasing awareness. 'I can remember how we went on a club crawl with the head of department and a few borough officials to show them what it was like. It was weird actually. We wanted to make it clear that club culture is something important, that we had to do away with prejudices – like the stories which go around about the clubs being full of drugs and weapons. It was also a matter of showing the CVs of the people running the clubs. These are often people who have previously studied art history or theatre. And of course we wanted to make them aware that clubbing is an economic growth factor.'

What influences the music industry in Berlin? This question was at the centre of her work, which she calls 'the promotion of economic development with cultural criteria'. Paradoxically, says Mühlhans, this is exactly why it has always been important to her that the clubs don't become too commercial. 'Anything which is too commercial loses its appeal. Once that happens it no longer stands out enough from what's going on in other cities.'

Viewed from this perspective, the whole MediaSpree affair has also been highly regrettable in economic terms. 'What should the borough do then?' asks Tanja Mühlhans, pointing out that the development plan is now in place and the contracts drawn up. Of course it would be better for the city if the clubs could stay; the city benefits considerably from its image precisely because the clubs are relatively uncommercial. But you have little hope of success, she says, if you stand there and protest once everything's signed and sealed. You have to get involved at the point when the decisions over the development plans are being made. 'But unfortunately none of the cool kids were there at that stage.'

That may be so, but the plans actually predate most of the clubs in the area. So who should have got involved? Nevertheless, some of the club promoters, such as the Bar 25 crew, have recognised this shortcoming: they were in attendance at the first meeting of the special committee which is examining the development options for the area.

However, there is actually another aspect which is more interesting than the question of what should have been done differently in the past: namely what city departments and the boroughs have learned from the MediaSpree debacle. According to Tanja Mühlhans, the authorities have started to change their way of thinking. One thing she's sure about is that every other borough going through a similar development process will make sure they involve all the parties who will be affected at an early stage. Furthermore, however, she believes that the era of planning on a grand scale is simply over. 'The world just moves too fast.' The inner-city boroughs must reserve spaces for future uses, she says: If they give it all away, at some point the city will be left with no possibilities for development.

This could actually signify a paradigm shift. Since the fall of the wall, Berlin's entire urban development has always revolved around the largest projects – understandably, given that the aim was to rebuild a city which had been divided for forty years and still showed signs of war damage. Who wouldn't have wanted to have a hand in these grand designs? It was the challenge of a lifetime, but the urban planners who were involved bit off much more than they could chew. None of the development goals set in the early nineties have been met. The city has not become a centre for trade with Eastern Europe, nor has its population risen significantly; the departure of old industries has not been stopped, and the new industries have not been able to compensate for these losses. What the city does have is a huge mountain of debt which will take decades to pay off. Furthermore, if you honestly measure the city's achievements today against the opportunities available after reunification, you can't say that the nineties were a spectacular period of urban development in Berlin.

The most interesting thing to emerge during this period is a concept which enjoyed a certain popularity in offbeat culture in particular, and which was practised by almost all clubs: the temporary use of spaces and buildings. At the point where nothing permanent was in place, where everything was in flux and no one knew exactly who actually owned a building or when funds would be available for renovation, many property developers turned over their spaces for a limited period to club promoters. The oft-quoted comment by Berlin's mayor Klaus Wowereit that Berlin is 'poor, but sexy' is basically nothing other than a philosophy of temporary use summed up in a catchphrase. There is no money left to implement large-scale projects, so we'll party in the buildings we have.

What we gonna do right here is go back

It's amazing how little trace the night life of the nineties has left on the city. Or perhaps not, given the fleeting nature of this nightly revelling. One of the central features of pop culture is that it's so short-lived. From the perspective of conservative culture critics, this is often misinterpreted as showing a lack of substance – how significant can a culture be when everything it considered right, true and beautiful the season before is thrown out with such merriment? Pop has always been able to live perfectly well with this criticism. But considering the effect that Berlin's night life has had, and continues to have, on the image of the city, the fact that the nightly goings on have made no visible impression is surprising.

You only have to take a short walk through the old club mile around the corner of Leipziger Straße and Wilhelmstraße. For several years this area saw constant streams of people on weekend nights: larger groups on their way to Tresor or E-Werk, smaller groups to Elektro or Friseur, two clubs which were direct neighbours on the corner of Mauerstraße and Kronenstraße. During the Love Parade the streets were sometimes closed off for hours on end because the clubs were full and there were simply too many people dancing on the street to music blaring out of car stereos. The original location of WMF was also here, and long after it had moved on people still used to regularly break into the disused building to hold illegal parties. That all ended when a couple of paranoid punks hanging around after an acid party threw beer bottles at police officers who were closing off the street. They weren't even planning to raid the building; they were just preparing for a marathon. After this the last remaining holes in the basement walls were carefully bricked up.

Nothing of these clubs has remained, although their disappearance has taken two different forms. The first kind is the complete disappearance, which culminates in the building being torn down. This happened not only to Tresor, but also to Elektro, a tiny club in the rooms of a former electrical supplies shop. A video installation by the artist Daniel Pflumm documents the demolition of the building.

The second and more common kind is a quiet disappearance whereby the club locations are simply converted back into normal buildings, offices which remain empty at night time. Their nightly excesses are consigned to a short chapter in their long history. This was the fate of 112 Leipziger Straße, the former Berlin branch of the household metalware manufacturer **Württembergische Metallwarenfabrik** which gave its name to the clubbing institution WMF, and of the building in Kronenstraße which was once home to Friseur. In exceptional cases a building's clubbing past lives on in a rudimentary form, as in the former E-Werk. The space was renovated after the club shut and serves as an occasional venue for events which try to borrow a certain glamour from the building's history.

The subcultural life of a city is always involved in its major urban developments, in the appreciation or depreciation of urban areas. The Manichaean struggle of the property developers versus the established residential population runs through the history of all the cool districts, and in most cases the traces of these disputes remain visible for a long time. Not on Leipziger Straße, however, due perhaps to the simple fact that only a small number of people lived or live in this area. In Berlin-Mitte in the nineties, the term 'eviction' most often meant that the period of temporary use was over and that the club would have to find a new location. So the promoters moved on and relinquished the area to the property developers, who left no trace of the buildings' past.

Perhaps one day people will regard the stone façade historicism of Leipziger Platz as the architectural signature of a decade in which the Berlin elites had the opportunity to reinvent their reunified city, but, caught between present delusions of grandeur and difficulties in coming to terms with the past, were unable to decide which way to go. Faced with the large sandy desert occupying this central part of the city, the planners said yes to the old street grid, but they also said yes to a few tower blocks. Tracks were laid for a tram which will probably never go into service, and at Potsdamer Platz, formerly the busiest square in Europe for road traffic, a replica of the very first set of traffic lights was installed.

The art of compromise was honed while the very real present of the nineties, the life being lived in this area throughout the period, was ignored. Then, once the famous red 'Info Box' offering views of the construction site was dismantled, the present, the time in which plans were drawn up and disputed, no longer had any architectural presence of its own.

As such, no building on Potsdamer Platz became a genuine child of its time or proud representative of the era in which it was built. No building tells a story of the nineties, that time of soaring spirits when the ruins of Berlin looked like they had once been constructed as the backdrop for a great adventure playground. The one exception might be the glazed roof of the Sony Centre, although for all its modernity it also houses the **Kaisersaal** (Emperor's Hall) of what used to be the Esplanade Grand Hotel. At great cost, the hall was moved by 75 metres because, although it was meant to bear witness to the past, in its original location it was unfortunately getting in the way. An absurd situation. Nevertheless, the reconstructed traffic lights are right where the original set were, before the almost 50-year period when nothing occupied this space at all except for a wall. There is little left to recall the wall's existence either, just three painted fragments at the entrance to the S-Bahn station and a line of cobblestones in the ground.

Risen from a ruin

It didn't have to be this way, at least not if it had been left to Dimitri Hegemann, founder of Tresor. In 1996, he came up with the idea of the Tresor Tower, a building which could have given Leipziger Platz an opportunity to bear witness to its past, if it had been built. The Tresor Tower was an attempt to build a memorial to techno. Hegemann's plan was to construct what he calls an 'image building' in the rooms above Tresor, which had already become a world-famous club. 'We had the idea of creating a platform here, a kind of start-up centre for everything which comes out of electronic music. Graphic design, fashion, music, philosophy, merchandising, a few shops. They could all have been based there. It would have been a top address which everyone knew; every taxi driver would have been able to point it out on a map and say, 'This is where our young intelligentsia resides. Between the Ministry of Finance, Sony and Daimler-Benz.'

The Italian architect Aldo Rossi drew up the initial plans. The property developers got on board. There was to be a radio station in Tresor Tower, plus apartments, and, as a second focus alongside the Tresor club, a huge concrete circus for the Cirque de Soleil.

'I asked around a bit, and realised that the thing would have been booked out immediately,' says Hegemann. 'We'd have kept the smaller room of Tresor, the old vault. And we'd have built an atrium. People would have gone clubbing, and while they were there they would have gone to get their hair cut or something to eat.' In short, the building would have been a worthy tribute to the Berlin of the nineties. Alas, it was not to be. Now the site is occupied by an empty property belonging to the insurance group Volksfürsorge.

There is reason to lament, then, even though the way things turned out doesn't appear to give Dimitri Hegemann any sleepless nights. Rather, it's with some amusement that he tells the story of when Volksfürsorge moved in. 'They told us they might have a little room at the back, and asked if we'd like to make a kind of lounge there and do it out in white leather. At that point I really thought, are you nuts?' Today, nothing on Leipziger Straße recalls that old Tresor which had seemed so indestructible. At a time when all other clubs had long-since moved on or perished, it still stood there solid as a rock. 'Tresor? Ah, they're still there,' remarked Blake Baxter with amusement and pride on his 2004 track 'What Happened?', a homage to countless techno clubs all over the world which had faded into history. Then, when it really **was** all over, people could hardly believe it – Tresor had existed for so long on the basis of temporary use, with three- and then two-month contracts, and announcements of its imminent closure had so often turned out to be false. The last party took place in May 2005 – after fifteen years, a remarkably long time. Tresor reopened in 2007, in an old power plant on Köpenicker Straße. The great bastion of old had arrived in the new club mile.

We meet a few hundred metres away in Markthalle on Pücklerstraße, one of several restaurants which Hegemann has helped to design. He says he's always enjoyed working with spaces.

Talking with Hegemann is an enjoyable experience, and not only because you get to hear stories of old heroes. Even now, at 53 years of age, he embodies an irresistible blend of enthusiasm, pragmatism and insatiable curiosity which never excludes those on the other side of the fence, but always incorporates them into his stories. After all, life goes on. There are not many people who have participated in as many different Berlin subcultures as Hegemann. He was part of eighties Kreuzberg with the band Einstürzende Neubauten and the Geniale Dilletanten festival; with Tresor he made his mark on the years of post-reunification euphoria, and he is also an active figure in the international clubbing capital which Berlin has become in the noughties.

'I was one of those little rebels who were dotted round the place and then all met up in Berlin – at the student administration office, or in Kreuzberg,' he says of his arrival in Berlin in the early eighties. 'People got together and worked on bringing about a new kind of awareness for this world which they had.'

In 1982 he organised the Atonal festival at the SO36 club, held four more times over the next ten years. He made contacts via the festival and travelled round the world, went to Sheffield, Chicago and Detroit, three cities which were to be of central importance for electronic dance music. He got to know the artists who influenced the techno scene. 'I didn't have a clue what was going on. I just flitted from one place to another. In Detroit someone handed me a tape by a band called Final Cut. Jeff Mills was one of the members. I didn't know about any of this, but that's how I found out about Underground Resistance. It was quite a turbulent time, and when I got back, the wall came down and we managed to get Tresor, I said to those solitary heroes in Detroit: hey, I have a stage for you here. And so they came, and I can still remember Blake Baxter saying, 'Man, I thought we were underground, but what you guys are doing over here…'

The Detroit-Berlin combination is one of the biggest strokes of luck in pop history. It was a collision of two very different paths. The afro-futurists from Detroit were looking to break away from the prescriptions of the American dance music business, while the East German youth was celebrating its new-found freedom. But the alliance which was formed proved to be exceedingly fruitful over a number of years. Jeff Mills, Robert Hood, Blake Baxter, Juan Atkins – all of the Detroit techno pioneers played in Tresor, and some of them even settled in Berlin for a while. The conceptual rigour which characterised the working method of the Detroit techno founders struck a chord in Germany which would continue to resonate for many years.

Tresor quickly became one of the most famous clubs in the world, partly because the eponymous label which Hegemann founded at an early stage gave the music worldwide exposure. For a while, the music played and released here was synonymous with techno itself: For a long time, Tresor's promotional slogan was 'True Spirit'.

Just like the old Tresor, the new one has two levels, with the Batterieraum up above and the 'vault', the **Tresor**, down below. Just as before, the club can be expanded into several adjoining rooms if necessary. One of these occasionally opened bars has a balcony with a wonderful view, not of a wooded area or the river, but of the expertly lit ruins of the old power plant – a strangely bleak cave-like landscape where industry becomes a surrogate nature.

In terms of its line-ups, too, the new Tresor has kept the faith. It continues to spin the traditional threads of techno and house which stretch all the way back to the club's beginnings. The crowd is surprisingly young, bearing in mind that Tresor is now the longest-running club in the city. Just as in the previous era, the average age is somewhere between 18 and 25, so this remains the favourite location for techno's eternal youth. Dimitri Hegemann is old enough to be their father. When Tresor celebrated its 18th birthday in 2009, there must have been some people in attendance who were entering adulthood at the same time as the club itself.

Those who got to know the old Tresor might forget where they are while dancing at the new venue, so striking are their similarities. That goes not only for the corridor you have to walk through to reach the dance floor, but also for some of the old, rusty safety deposit boxes which have found their way here from the old club. The iron bars also resemble those from the old Tresor. The whole place is a little more spacious; the room is set up slightly differently; the bar is in a different place, but otherwise… it's a curious experience.

After all, the fascinating thing about Tresor – apart from the music – was always the way a certain attitude was translated into architecture. This was even implied by the name. Previously Berlin's clubs were called things like Planet and UFO, names which denoted an escape, a desire to lose oneself in outer space. This feeling was still firmly rooted in the cramped environment of the eighties when the wall was still standing.

Indeed, after the wall came down, there were acres of space all of a sudden. The East had been opened up and with it all those deserted buildings ready to be occupied and used. With its very name, Tresor ('vault') conveyed that something new was beginning here: the misappropriation of these discovered locations, their transformation into something else.

All the clubs in the area named themselves in the same way: Friseur used to be a hairdresser, E-Werk was an electricity substation, WMF was a household metalware manufacturer and Elektro was an electrical supplies shop – in all these places a sense of astonishment at the real history of the buildings went hand in hand with the pleasure of appropriating the locations. It also had something of the old 'do it yourself' punk principle about it. History had washed up this space at your feet, and now it was a matter of making it your own somehow. Nowhere was this accomplished as brilliantly as in Tresor, which made a dance floor out of the vault of the legendary Wertheim department store. The great and tragic history of this property (established by a Jewish family, it was 'Aryanised' by the Nazis, badly damaged by bombs in 1943, then 'Socialised' by the East German authorities, who in the mid-1950s demolished the ruins, except for a small section containing the vault, to clear the 'death strip' behind the wall) was transcended in a great dialectical movement and transported into the joyous moments of this dance floor lodged between the safety deposit boxes.

In fact, the names of the clubs on the new club mile also give you a clue as to how they think of themselves. They too play on their locations, but in a different way to before. Berghain took its two syllables from Kreuzberg and Friedrichshain, Watergate refers to its geographical location on the waterside and next to a bridge, and so does Bar 25, which has simply turned its house number into its name. But whereas the old names conveyed surprise, the new ones are relatively matter-of-fact statements.

Of course, the fact that the new Tresor has installed a few of its old safety deposit boxes in its new basement to evoke a particular feeling on the dance floor makes perfect sense in marketing terms. Nevertheless, it feels a bit like a defeat; as though Tresor, too, has switched over to that new Berlin historicism which puts the remaining pieces of history together as best it can. The main difference between putting safety deposit boxes in the basement of a power plant to simulate the good old nineties basement feeling and rebuilding the Berlin City Palace is the scale of the project. For the **Stadtschloss**, too, is meant to cover up a loss, to defy the trials and tribulations of the twentieth century which destroyed so much more than the historic centre of the city.

Yet perhaps this is going too far – after all, we're just talking about a few steel boxes in the basement of a huge building complex. The club only takes up a fraction of the space, perhaps one tenth. The rest is still empty, but Hegemann wouldn't be Hegemann if he didn't already have a few plans and ideas brewing. He envisages additional club rooms focusing on different themes, and an exhibition hall. 'I'm against the mainstream. The interesting things are always those which are against something,' he says, in conclusion to the interview. 'Something new has to be developed in order to rebel against all the crap.'

Back to concrete

What's left? This is always the wrong question to ask when you're talking about culture. It's always those who come along next who decide what remains, and by the time the preservationists turn up, the DJs have long since left the building. Berlin's night life has always been mobile; it migrates. Since the fall of the wall it has relocated from the city centre to the border between Kreuzberg and Friedrichshain.

In retrospect it's amazing that it took so long for Berliners in general, and the clubbing crowd in particular, to discover the banks of the Spree and to mark the area on their mental map of the city. That's not to say that nothing ever happened here at night. There were a whole load of illegal clubs on the waterside, the most run-down of which was probably an after-party location calling itself Deli, of all things, that could be found for a while where Maria now is. Deli was furnished somewhat differently, however. There was nothing but a ghetto blaster and a campfire in the middle of the room with a few buzzing individuals crouched around it. For a couple of years, there was also a trailer park behind the Eastside Gallery (a remaining section of the wall) where a few British techno punks lived.

But Berlin's self-discovery after the fall of the wall was primarily directed towards its central urban districts: Potsdamer Platz and Alexanderplatz were treated as public spaces and historic sites; the residential districts of Mitte, Prenzlauer Berg and Friedrichshain as huge pools of cheap living space; and the abandoned industrial or commercial properties as potential party locations and exhibition spaces. It was only around the turn of the century that individual entrepreneurs began setting up the famous beach bars on abandoned waterfront sites.

Yet the clubs will not be able to stay forever either; the first signs of migration are already becoming visible. They're being drawn back into the city, particularly to Kreuzberg, a district which took a long time to recover from the fall of the wall. In the eighties it had been an unrivalled centre for people who wanted to reinvent themselves and live a life of leisure, but its slow pace of life could hardly compete with the vitality of East Berlin in the nineties, either in the daytime or at night. In the meantime, though, the dust clouds have long-since settled in the area between Kastanienallee and Hackescher Markt, and Mitte has become ensnared in a nostalgia which closely resembles Kreuzberg's longing for the eighties: ah, the nineties, the great era when anything seemed possible here!

That's not to say that Kreuzberg has a great deal more going on than Mitte, but it has enough. The constant-erosion-of-free-spaces blues became a smash hit long ago, and it always fits, just like the classic about the ever-widening divide between rich and poor. Of course, the fact that everyone's singing it doesn't make it wrong. However, the amount of insight gained is limited. How good do things have to be? The wall isn't going to fall for a second time, and if you allow your gaze to drift beyond the Berlin horizon, you quickly realise that the conditions the German capital offers for ravers are still ideal. Everyone basically knows this, too: the cost of living is low, and there is still no sign of the kind of economic development which would attract tens of thousands of job-seekers to Berlin. So the rents are going to stay cheap, and the already proverbial 'rich Swedes' can't buy up so many apartments that it would change this situation substantially.

Besides, not everything was easy in the nineties either. At the start of the decade there was a massive shortage of affordable apartments; the prices were a good deal higher than they are today. It was post-reunification fever and its wild growth forecasts which gave scores of property developers the idea that there must be a fortune to be made in Berlin. The idea came to nothing. On the contrary, the oversupply of housing caused prices to tumble – a stroke of luck comparable to that of the low-cost flights, which of course were not brought about by kind-hearted airlines choosing to fly Europe's youth to Berlin for a weekend of raving at rock-bottom prices. It was a case of cut-throat competition. Each airline will underbid the other until the competitor has nothing left in the tank. This is another one of the variables which, in combination, have helped Berlin become the vibrant city that it is.

So many languages here: Thursday

There are moments in Berlin night life when it would be nice to be a native English speaker, just to be able to appreciate all the nuances. Like when a Swede and a Spaniard who have just met in Watergate and shared a taxi to Alexanderplatz talk about how great they think Berlin is: 'I fucking love this city.' Or shortly afterwards in the lift when a Dutch guy who lives in London gets talking to a Norwegian girl, and she's there with a friend who just moved to London. While they're attempting to explain all of this – they do have fifteen floors to travel – another Norwegian chips in, telling the Dutch guy that, should he ever travel to Norway, he mustn't go to Bergen as it's incredibly boring. Then we reach the top. The door opens and the lift operator lets everyone out. On his way out of the lift, a guy in his late twenties who sounds as if he might come from Australia, and who has been listening to his companions' conversation the whole way, says, 'Norway, Norway – that's the country with the fjords, right?'

We're at Weekend on Alexanderplatz, one of the city's most beautiful clubs. It extends over three floors of the 'Haus des Reisens' tower, built between 1969 and 1971 for the 'Headquarters of the Travel Agency of the German Democratic Republic' and for offices of the GDR airline Interflug. It's 65 metres high, has seventeen floors, has only been partially renovated and is not protected as a historic monument. This explains why there is often talk of one of the 150-metre-high tower blocks being built here which, according to local government plans, were meant to be standing long ago. If an investor were to show an interest. This has not been the case to date, but that means we have Weekend instead.

When the club opened in 2004 it caused quite a sensation. At first it took up only the twelfth floor where, with windows on three sides, you could look out over the city as you danced. The walk-around bar, extremely elegant lighting and slightly retro charm of this administrative building with its glazed entrance combined to great effect. When all the lights went out at the peak of a night, leaving the club lit up only by the surrounding city, the effect was unparalleled. In 2007 the fifteenth floor was completed: a slightly smaller room which afforded itself the luxury, in spite of the view, of blacking out all its windows (some have since been uncovered again). The interior lighting was also fairly minimal, except for a spectacular wall of spotlights. Added to this was a roof terrace, another rather masterful piece of club design, with a bar inset into the floor and a glazed safety barrier around the building's edge. That meant no bar staff or bottles would get in the eye line of guests who wished to look out over the city. Tonight just the 15th floor and the roof are open; it's mid-July 2008 and people are packed onto the dance floor like sardines.

Certain sharp-tongued observers claim that the actual Berlin party community, the people who form the hard core of the city's night life, consists of just three of four hundred people in total, counting all the clubs, while everyone else is just visiting. When you look around Weekend tonight, the theory doesn't seem entirely implausible. There are a couple of dozen people who clearly set themselves apart; they're the Berliners. They're gathered near the DJ booth, partly because they came here to dance, and partly because they know the DJs. They're a few years older and clearly less dolled up than the other guests, whose clothing does not adhere to the understated principle of the Berlin scene. The non-Berlin girls wear short skirts and shoes with high heels; the guys are sporting expensive jeans and polo shirts.

Fritz Zander and Sven von Thülen organise this night which happens once a month. The pair have made several records together in recent years (as Zander VT), and von Thülen has worked as an editor of the music magazine **De:Bug**. For this Thursday night they've invited Phillip Sollmann as a guest DJ. He's achieved a certain amount of fame over the past two or three years, both as a producer and a DJ, under the name Efdemin. One of the night's surprising moments reveals how fundamentally this crowd has overridden the coolness code of Berlin night life:

'Are you Efdemin?' two German lads ask Sollmann as he goes to smoke a couple of cigarettes on the roof terrace before he plays. 'Yeah, why?' – 'Man, you're the best DJ in the world!' says one of them, and adds, turning to his friend, 'Man, Efdemin, no fucking way!' Then to Sollmann, 'Hey mate, what time are you on?' – 'In half an hour' – 'Wicked, can we have a photo of you?' – 'Do you have to? Can't we wait until after, when I'm playing?' – 'Yeah, sure, cool mate.' Now a girl who's sitting next to us joins in. 'Hey, are you famous?' Sollmann laughs. The girl continues: 'They're all talking about you, so you must be famous. I'm just drunk.' At this point she flings herself back onto the sofa. Then a Swede plonks himself in front of us. 'Anybody got drugs? Ecstasy? Cocaine? I don't care.' No one answers and he goes away again. The two Efdemin fans are still standing there. Somehow they can't find the right way to retire from the exchange graciously, so they stare at us and repeat themselves a couple more times: 'Fuck me. Efdemin, man. Fucking hell.' At some point they do toddle off, only to reappear soon afterwards to ask Sollmann if he can put them on the guestlist the next time he plays. Later they can be seen dancing directly in front of the booth, throwing their arms in the air at every breakdown. One of them is wearing a Pete Doherty hat and a hoodie, the other has blond hair and is wearing his trousers low. The summer holidays have just begun.

If you wanted to quickly put your finger on what the Easyjet set is then tonight you'd just have to look at the two French guys, around twenty years old, who order a champagne bucket full of ice at the bar, then cram it with seven cans of Red Bull and a bottle of vodka. They pay with a large note, and either they're very drunk or very generous; in any case they've disappeared by the time the barman comes back with a handful of small notes and coins. The music critic Simon Reynolds once described the British rave movement of the early nineties as 'mass bohemia on E'. Tonight at Weekend you can't resist the notion that the early noughties equivalent would have to be 'mass jet set on vodka and Red Bull'. Not so many people here have obviously taken drugs. Where would they have got them from anyway? The vast majority of the guests are weekend trippers, and if there's one consequence of the airlines' increased security measures, it's that people don't even think about stuffing drugs down their socks. They can't buy any on the way to the hotel, either, so they go without. Instead, they pour vodka and Red Bull down their necks. An interesting combination – it gets you ridiculously drunk whilst keeping you fully alert and pumped up. Perfect if you want to really let your hair down. The term 'mass jet set' also fits because flying from one party to another used to be a sign of wealth, whereas now the descendents of French aristocrats have to share this privilege with the sons of Irish labourers and daughters of Swedish nurses.

Another interesting thing is the dance floor. The term 'handbag house' once surfaced in the nineties, a derogatory name for fluffy house music which was employed to poke fun at the musical preference of a particular inner-city after-work club culture – of secretaries who piled their handbags on the dance floor and danced around them. Just like a whole group of girls in their early twenties at Weekend tonight. It looks cute, and vaguely reminds me of Interrail tourists of earlier decades who stacked up their rucksacks on train platforms so they could sit around and smoke joints. However, there's no handbag house to be heard here (nor its German equivalent, 'hairdresser electro'). The DJ is playing minimal house, which is anything but 'secretary music'. Looking at the crowd, it's hard to decide whether they're massively up for a big night, or if they're simply not fussed what comes out of the speakers. At any rate, they're dancing like crazy.

When we leave at half past four the dance floor is rocking like there's no tomorrow. The lift operator is reading a book on the way down; the entrance is deserted. Two lone door staff are standing in front of the entrance keeping watch. There are a good dozen taxis waiting out on the street.

Golden Gate is a couple of hundred metres down the road in a bend in the S-Bahn tracks by Jannowitzbrücke station. It's one of those places which tend to sail in the slipstream of other clubs. WMF used to be nearby; both it and Golden Gate have been through several closures and reopenings in their time. At the moment Golden Gate has just started up again – and it's going quite well by the looks of things. It's shortly before five on a Friday morning, not long now until the commuter traffic starts rolling across the huge crossroads in front of the entrance, while in here everyone's just getting into their groove.

There are no vodka-red-bull-fuelled tourists in their early twenties here, however. The crowd is a little older, late twenties to late thirties. It's more a case of clubbing veterans who get by as freelancers and therefore don't have to think about the next morning. Computer programmers, people who close off streets for film productions, other assorted drifters. The music is house with a gritty edge, and it's rather loud, though no one is dancing. Amongst the noise, however, everyone is feeling pretty good and shouting conversation into their neighbour's ear.

Golden Gate is a small club with its own very unique charm which stems from its utter decrepitude. It's entirely surrounded by traffic of varying degrees of volume: above is the S-Bahn, below the U-Bahn, all around are cars. Basically, you're having a party in the structural support of a bridge. And then there's the garden. It's hard to imagine a starker contrast to the terrace of Weekend, which is tastefully proportioned with parasols and wooden decking. This place has lots of dirt, old camping furniture, temporary barriers separating it from the street, yet more dirt, trampled out cigarette butts all over the place and an old hiking boot in the corner. It looks like a bomb hit a couple of weeks ago and no one's done much about it. It feels like it did in the early nineties.

It's shortly before six o'clock when we leave. The city is waking up, the first delivery vans are sending out their goods. On the way home we go past the entrance to Weekend again. The last guests are just leaving. There are completely normal offices on the building's other floors. Soon the cleaning crew will be here to wipe down the lift, throw away the cigarette butts and discarded flyers and rearrange the foyer, which has spent the night as a cloakroom.

The Easyjet set
and Europe's new clubbing geography

Every weekend thousands of techno tourists fly to Berlin to have the kind of party they can't experience at home. Many DJs and producers have moved over here. The low-cost airlines have revolutionised clubbing.

Aeroplanes as taxis – the most fitting symbol for the Easyjet rave culture doesn't come from Easyjet itself, but from a competitor. The entire fleet of Germania, the low-cost subsidiary of Hapag-Lloyd, is painted yellow with a chequered stripe on the side: a reference to New York's yellow cabs. For a while, Germania also advertised its flight prices as 'taxi fares'. A taxi ride to another city – what was still the preserve of the rich and eccentric ten years ago has now become a normality in Europe. Anyone who books early enough can fly from one city to another, if not for a taxi fare then still for well under a hundred euros, leaving on a Friday and coming back on the Monday. What makes it such a fitting symbol, however, is that the taxi is the preferred mode of transport for people going out clubbing. Anyone who wants to really let loose will leave their car and bike at home. This is precisely how the Easyjet set came about: every weekend thousands take a taxi flight to Berlin, because you can party here like in no other major European city.

The Easyjet ravers are the defining element of European clubbing culture in the noughties. They came, without any great fanfare, and developed into one of the most important subcultural groups of the present time. Their significance is huge. They have fundamentally altered Europe's club geography. In view of their enormous influence, it's astounding that Easyjet ravers were the chance offspring of two essentially unrelated developments: the liberalisation of European air travel and the emergence of the low-cost airlines, on the one hand, and the economic ruin of the city of Berlin on the other. The former devalued air travel: rather than being an expensive luxury, jetting off to a European city for the weekend is now a budget treat for the masses. City tourism has become a mass phenomenon, hence the standard of service, which is no better than in the second class of an intercity train. Berlin's economic downturn is the sad result of an overly optimistic budget forecast made in the early nineties. At the time, the parameters put in place for the future development of the capital were meant to produce a flourishing metropolis within a few years. None of these expectations were fulfilled, however. As a result, Berlin, a city with three and a half million residents but which is designed for around five million, didn't grow – it shrank. This meant that the industrial wasteland and disused buildings in central locations remained as they were. And of course, there was already a party scene in place which had learned, in the nineties, how to make temporary clubs and parties out of these spaces.

The Berlin Airport Company made the best out of this situation of economic distress. Tegel and Schönefeld airports may not be important hubs of international air travel like Frankfurt or Munich. However, for a number of years, the airport operators have been making sure that a larger share of the airlines which land here, compared with other cities, are low-cost airlines. The fact that these two Berlin airports combined constitute Germany's third-largest airport, in terms of passenger numbers, is due simply to an above-average proportion of low-cost airlines landing here. Air Berlin has a large base at Tegel; thousands of people make a beeline for it every day. More important than Tegel, however, is Schönefeld Airport, which has recorded an astonishing rate of growth over recent years: from 1.7 million passengers in 2003 to 6.3 million in 2007. And eighty percent of these passengers fly with a low-cost airline. Easyjet has a huge base in Schönefeld. In summer 2008 the airline proudly announced that, for the first time, it had checked in around half of all the passengers who landed in Schönefeld – that's around 330,000 people. Of course, there are no statistics to show how many of them come to Berlin to go clubbing. But an estimate of 10,000 low-cost airline passengers in Berlin's clubs each weekend couldn't be too far off the mark.

The consequences are profound. If you stand in the queue of any Berlin club, any night of the week, a good half of the people waiting with you will be from abroad. You'll hear English, French, Italian, Spanish, and these are people who have flown to Berlin for the weekend to go clubbing. You can talk to any Berlin club promoter – all of them admit, whether openly or with some reserve, that around one in three clubs would have to close if you were to take away the Easyjet ravers.

It would be wrong to imagine the Easyjet set as a discrete, or even a homogenous, subculture. It's simply a subset of the subcultures which have emerged out of house and techno – a load of people from all over the place who love music. And if you go to the garish orange Easyjet section of Schönefeld Airport and take a look at the passengers streaming into the arrivals hall, you won't see anything which distinguishes those who you'll be meeting on a dance floor later from the rest.

The Easyjet ravers are people like Anna, a Danish student in her early twenties. I meet her in front of Rotation Records on Weinbergsweg. Anna is standing by the door having a cigarette while her boyfriend listens to some records in the shop. She's had a look at the T-shirts hanging in the entrance of the shop and she's sat and waited for a while on the sofa. She's bored. I ask her if she wants to go for a coffee, she lets her boyfriend know and we go to a café on the other side of the street. It's a Friday afternoon in September; they arrived from Copenhagen on Thursday evening. There are four of them – her, her boyfriend, and two other friends. They're staying in a flat which the parents of some friends have bought in Kreuzberg. It's the first time she's been to Berlin. She can't really say what expectations she has of the city. She's curious, she says. On Sunday I meet her again, on Kastanienallee. It's the afternoon and they're just leaving the flea market. She and her friends went to Watergate on Friday, which she says was 'great', and they stayed there until the early hours of the morning. On Saturday they wanted to go to Berghain, but the queue was too long, so they went to Bar 25, but they didn't get in there, so they went back to Watergate again. Then they sat for a while on the banks of the Spree.

Michele from Milan could also be called an Easyjet raver. I get talking to him in the queue for Berghain. He's in his late twenties and it's not his first time in Berlin. He's been coming regularly for a couple of years, he says, always just for a couple of days, and always involving a healthy dose of clubbing. He loves the Berlin minimal sound; the label Perlon made a particular impression on him. Later I meet him again at the bar and he tells me that he actually wanted to come to Berlin for a couple of weeks in the summer, but it didn't work out unfortunately; he had to stay in Italy because of his job. He's a software programmer and his working rhythm is dictated by projects, so he has periods of very intense work and deadlines to meet which are followed by more relaxed periods. He takes advantage of these to visit Berlin – it doesn't have to be Berlin, though; he goes to other cities too.

The Easyjet set consists of people like the techno DJ from Avignon who flies to Berlin every couple of months because he has the feeling that the clubs here embody a different spirit, and that he has to expose himself to this environment on a regular basis so that he doesn't lose his orientation (or something like that – we were at the bar in Watergate and anything but sober). Or the two Swiss guys in Bar 25 who flew in from Zurich and definitely want to buy some drugs, or at least swap some. Thousands of Easyjet ravers populate the city's clubs, and each of them has their own story. Everyone who lives in Europe and loves house and techno has made a trip to Berlin at some point in the last ten years. Everyone.

The techno hostel

And all these people need a place to stay. Indeed, the hostels which are springing up all over the central districts are the most visible sign of how the Easyjet set is changing the face of the city. If you've paid just a few euros for your flight, you don't want to spend much on accommodation either. You can stay here for 15 to 20 euros a night. The Circus was one of the first hostels to target this new clientele. It opened in 2001 and can be found at Rosenthaler Platz in the Mitte district, a traffic junction where four streets, a U-Bahn line, two trams and the bus all meet. Since autumn 2008, The Circus has occupied two corner buildings: the main hostel on Weinbergsweg and the extension over the road on Torstraße.

Andreas Becker is the founder of The Circus. The hostel's history, he says, is closely tied in with Berlin club culture. He opened his first hostel, with 28 beds, in 1997. Just like most of the clubs of that era, he says, the hostel was born out of the temporary use culture of the nineties. The housing association allocated him a building on Reinhardtstraße on the corner of Am Zirkus (hence the name), opposite what is now the headquarters of the Free Democratic Party. This was rent free for one year on the condition that he renovate it himself. The building was in disrepair, so Becker got to work. From that point on, he says, it was 'growth, growth, growth' all the way. He says that, through the hostel, he feels associated with the people behind Berghain. Just like the club, his hostel made the transition from a project into an established enterprise which accepts the mechanisms of a normal business, but nevertheless tries to remain true to, and indeed celebrate, its own roots. Today The Circus has 240 beds, two thirds of which are in dorms, one third in private rooms. The second building, on the other side of the junction, is more of a budget hotel than a hostel. It has another 140 beds, all in private rooms.

We have a conversation in The Circus's meeting room. Next to us are a few employees sitting at computers managing the bookings; a scent of potato soup is wafting in from a small kitchen; on a table by the wall are a pair of decks and a mixer. Circus is in partnership with Rotation Records, a small record shop located a few doors further down Weinbergsweg.

Scores of well-known DJs buy records here, and there's a lot of passing custom. Nikolaus Schäfer, co-owner of Rotation, used to work at The Circus, and one of The Circus's shareholders is Rotation's other owner. If the way things normally work is for tourists to gradually discover the institutions of the scene once they've arrived, for Rotation it was quite the opposite: the shop began as a child of the hostel, the idea being to offer the clubbing tourists the opportunity to take a couple of records home with them from their trip. At first Rotation also served as an internet café for the hostel guests. That was in 2003. Now the shop is an integral part of the Berlin techno scene.

Interview with a hostel philosopher

With Andreas Becker you could talk at length and in detail about every aspect of the hostel business and clubbing tourism. He is 41 years old and he came to Berlin from Westphalia at the end of the eighties. He started studying, to no great success, and ended up packing a rucksack and embarking on lengthy trips. After a few years he came back to Berlin, he says, and worked in a sex shop in a squat in Prenzlauer Berg. An acquaintance from the squat persuaded him to put his travelling experiences to use and open his own hostel. At the time, says Becker, there were roughly 400 beds available in Berlin in the budget price range – aside from the youth hostels. That was ten years ago. Now there are 18,000. What does the hostel philosopher have to say about this?

In the first six or seven years, the hostels couldn't expand quickly enough to keep up with the growth of the market. A place would open up and after two days it would be full. There was a permanent shortage of beds, at least for six to eight months of the year, which is enough to make a reasonable profit. This has changed over the last three years or so. The first problem which emerged was the pressure on prices, which haven't evolved here the same way as in the rest of Europe. The first factor was that you could find a cheap bed any time, even in mid-summer. That's why prices haven't gone up like they have in London or Amsterdam. They've even started dropping from what was already a very low level. Basically, the hostels in Berlin are in the same situation as the luxury hotels: there's a surplus of supply. This means we have the highest European standards at prices which are among the lowest in Western Europe. Even the prices in major Eastern European cities like Budapest and Prague have exceeded those in Berlin for the last two years.

What kind of people come and stay at your hostels?

That has completely changed. Like everything in the hostel sector. At first our guests were classic backpackers. They had a couple of pictures of the city in their minds: Berlin, the Nazi city; Berlin, the city with the wall. These images were then linked, in the backpackers' minds, to certain tourist sights. But it wasn't as if these people had sought out a particular city to visit.

It was about being away?

Exactly. They're travelling; every city has its own cliché. In the evening they'd come to the reception and ask where they could go to get a drink around here. Then the low-cost airlines started linking up Europe, and that's when the entire clientele changed. More and more people started flying to Berlin for three days from Madrid, Paris or London – the most prominent were the English; they're the dominant group in rave tourism. They come to Berlin for a specific purpose and know exactly what they want to do when they get here. They've already planned to go to Panoramabar on Friday night because a certain DJ is on, then on Saturday they want to go to Weekend because some other DJ they're interested in is playing there, and then they'll go back to Berghain. They've found out what's happening on the internet in advance – they no longer have to come to the reception to ask what's going on in the evening.

It's a very specialised form of tourism.

It's particularly noticeable amongst the English, the Italians and the Spanish. Of course, this results in a different perception of the city. Berlin is no longer the city of the wall, of the Nazis, or of Hitler. It offers a destination for a precisely defined group of people with a very distinct profile of requirements. Berlin is the city which provides techno-lovers with the largest and highest-quality selection of DJs – and at very low prices. The same thing goes for the art aficionados. For them, there are more galleries and events than can be taken in on a single trip, also at very low prices. The third group which mustn't be forgotten is the gay tourists. For 30 million gay Europeans, Berlin is the city which is most libertine in its sexual attitudes – along with Amsterdam, perhaps – and one which offers a massive range of sex clubs.

There are parties for every kind of fetish, it's incredibly cheap, and the door policies are not at all strict. I would call it functional tourism. Everyone gets a very precise dose of music, art or sex, depending on their preferences.

So can we see the emergence of a new European clubbing geography?

Yes, absolutely. The catchment area of a city's night life has expanded to cover the entire continent. This is also linked to social changes. We're living in an age of social differentiation. This new tourism is not a mass phenomenon for the time being. Not just any John Smith from Manchester will now be flying to Berlin on a regular basis to go clubbing. But if John Smith is into techno and goes out a lot in Manchester, then he'll no longer restrict his nights out to Manchester or perhaps London; he'll come over to Berlin as well. Of course, this applies in exactly the same way to other subcultures. Specialised lifestyles can include anything at all, computer games for instance. There are conventions all over Europe which gamers fly to in order to play with or against one another. The same goes for other scenes. The gay, party-loving Ryanair customers no longer just go out in their home country; they fly to three or four Gay Prides, Rainbow Parades or Christopher Street Days. We can see Europe moving closer together. The differentiation of lifestyles is combining with the evolution of travel possibilities. You can see it. You can feel it.

It becomes a mass movement when you add the various individual movements together.

Certainly. Take Berghain. This is a club which has a legendary reputation amongst our guests. On a good night there are 3,000 people there. A good half of them have travelled from Tel Aviv, Manchester, Barcelona or wherever else. And most of these 1,500 people have flown over for precisely that reason. Just for that. There are entirely new movements emerging. Of course, this is also influenced by the internet; it adds fuel to the process. You find like-minded people online, and the low-cost airlines then allow you to meet up in a certain place. You don't have to know one another beforehand; it's enough if you're into the same music. But if you put all these people together, then it adds up to a mass movement. You can see that here, because this is where they meet.

How will the situation develop?

The debate about increasing the cost of flying made the market nervous for a while – that's the question as to whether the fuel for flights should be taxed at a higher rate out of consideration for the environment. This could have pushed prices up so far as to put this business model in danger. But the politicians moved away from the idea. In the end the conviction prevailed that low-cost flying is part of our lifestyle, that it should be accepted as such and that we mustn't fight it. The price increases now under discussion are in the region of ten to twenty euros per ticket. The market will be able to absorb this.

What effect does it have when flying becomes part of daily life?

This kind of tourism used to be restricted to a relatively small circle of people: rich Western Europeans and North Americans. This circle is expanding – in the case of Western Europe, to huge swathes of the population. But they are also being joined by rich Asians, Africans and Eastern Europeans, and the middle classes from these areas will come too, in time. This means that the number of people coming over here will multiply. Travel has emerged as one of the most important status symbols in society. There's no reason why the numbers should start to decrease. Tourism will continue to grow.

This has knock-on effects for the city. The area around The Circus, for instance, has changed considerably in recent years. Before the hostel opened, Rosenthaler Platz was a draughty traffic junction with a sex shop and three kebab shops. Today there's some kind of commerce in almost every building: there are several laundrettes; a café where no one reads the paper any more, but all the customers have a laptop in front of them; and several restaurants and takeaways. You can hear any European language at any time of day or night. What's more, Becker explains, many visitors simply don't go home. Around forty of the hundred or so employees at The Circus were originally guests who ended up staying. Many of them now live in the area.

The Easyjet DJ

If it hadn't been for tourism, the entire European rave culture as it evolved in the nineties would never have come about. Acid house, the soundtrack of the 'Summer of Love' of 1987, may have been a musical import from Chicago, but the cultural mechanisms which turned this music into a massive party were developed by British DJs who spent the summer in Ibiza. Then they brought this culture back to England.

Indeed, today's rave tourism is not just about those who visit the clubs and love the music. Low-cost flying has also altered the DJ's job description. If you wanted to get booked to play all over Europe in the nineties, you had to be a pretty big name. Otherwise there was no way of covering the costs of being flown over for one club night. If you weren't a big star, you played in clubs which you could get to by car or by train.

That has fundamentally changed now. Equally, for club promoters who book DJs to play for around 500 euros – i.e. those in the broad mid-range of the DJ market – it's worthwhile flying the artists over. Previously they would have looked to see who was available from their own city or region. Now it's a matter of which DJ in Europe they'd like to book – the cost of the flights only represents a small portion of the running costs.

This has other consequences. When it's so cheap and easy to fly all over Europe, your home city becomes less important for your own bookings. You no longer have to live in the place where you play. This means that many DJs are able to move to Berlin even if they earn their money by performing elsewhere. Plus, living in Berlin is not only cheap, you also have the feeling of having your finger on the pulse. For some DJs, the fact that they're living in Berlin even increases their market value.

This has had huge consequences in recent years. Several hundred DJs, producers and label managers have moved to Berlin: Richie Hawtin, Ricardo Villalobos, Magda, Troy Pierce, Ewan Pearson, DJ Hell, Matthew Edwards alias Radio Slave, Jerome Sydenham, Matthew Styles, Jesse Rose, Alejandra Iglesias alias Dinky, Tyree Cooper, Dasha Rush, Daniel Bell, Dan Curtin, Jay Haze, Margaret Dygas, Mike Shannon, Samim, Alan Abrahams alias Portable, Lee Jones, Daniel Wang, Guillaume Coutu, The Mole, Seth Troxler – the list goes on and on. Luciano came and then moved on to Switzerland in 2007. The sub_static label moved from Cologne to Berlin, as did Sender Records; Perlon left Frankfurt for Berlin, just like the managers of Get Physical; Jeremy Caulfield relocated his Dumb Unit label from Toronto to Berlin. Whereas in the nineties the scene was still divided between several different centres throughout the world, including cities such as Chicago, New York, London, Manchester, Sheffield, Paris, Frankfurt and Cologne, today it's largely concentrated in Berlin. The collapse of the American rave scene and the cultural conservatism of the Bush era have surely also played a role in the decision of so many US citizens to emigrate to Berlin. But it's not just Americans. Techno activists from all over Europe have moved over to Berlin, and those who haven't moved over at least have a room to stay in. For it's not only cheap to live in Berlin, it's also cheap to travel here, and to get away again.

Where do you live, techno?

Andrew Rasse is one of many who have moved to Berlin. He came to Germany from St. Louis in 2007. He's a producer, DJ and label manager. Alphahouse is the name of his record label; he brought it with him to Berlin. Butane is the alias under which he produces minimal techno. The first thing Rasse mentions when asked why he moved here is that Berlin is the techno capital of the world. This is the reason that so many people from all over the world have come here, he says – there's a stable scene to welcome people like him. 'Before I moved here I could have given you a list of a hundred or so people that I could have called to do me a favour. That's unique. I don't know any other city that offers that.'

The second reason is that Berlin acts as a hub: 'I have my workshop here, my studio, my office. I fly in and out, it's cheap, the people are nice; living here can be pleasantly non-committal.' Thirdly, he says, it's a city where you can get along in everyday life without speaking the language. In Tokyo, just having to go to the visa office would be a struggle. In Berlin, he says, he can complete all the tasks that are necessary for his daily life in English, even his taxes. The fourth thing, says Rasse, is that Berlin is one of the world's most beautiful cities – at least in summer. He can't think of any major city in the world where life is so relaxed. The fifth reason is that the dance culture to which he feels such an allegiance enjoys greater recognition here than it does in the USA. Besides, the gigs which earn him money are all in Europe. Interestingly, he adds, you even get more bookings in the USA if you've had some success in Europe. 'Then all of a sudden people are saying, "Oh he's a professional DJ in Berlin!" They treat me with respect.'

It's a crazy world that the migrant workers of modern subculture like Andrew Rasse inhabit. A world with an extremely relative concept of home: you live in Berlin, but the main bits of the city you know are the clubs, your own street and a few restaurants. Most of the people you come into contact with are in the business of playing music somewhere in the world every weekend, just like you are. Only a few make the effort to learn German. One reason is that it's not really worth the effort – all Germans speak English, after all.

Rasse studied philosophy and is an avid reader, with an interest in both arts and sciences. He also analyses himself very closely. When asked how this way of life could be described, he thinks for a moment and then says, 'Everyone has a different story, but certain things apply to everyone. The music business is a shitty business. You're only as good as your last record. There's always this uncertainty. I may just dry up one day. You can't force people to like your music. I feel fortunate that people do. I'm very lucky and feel flattered that I'm invited to play all over the world. But that may not last forever. One day I might be irrelevant. What then? Will I continue to live here? Where am I gonna go? There's this series of small walls that you build for yourself to not let yourself get too comfortable here. Because it can be a temporary thing. Nobody is really sure of how sustainable this is as a career. How permanent is a job which involves going to Panoramabar at nine o'clock on a Sunday morning and getting drunk when you want to meet up with your colleagues? It's all pretty crazy. I live totally comfortably at the moment, but who knows what's around the corner; who knows what will be going on in two years. I don't want to end up a 35-year-old has-been. In that case, I'd rather do something else.'

When we meet, Rasse is living in the district of Friedrichshain and is about to move into a larger apartment. His approach to accommodation, he says, is the same as his approach to the German language: in order not to feel too at home, he's lived for the whole time in an apartment without a living room.

It probably takes a period of five years, he adds, before you feel at home in Berlin. He explains that one of his friends who has been in Berlin for this long and who has a German girlfriend is now learning German. He'd been here so long, this friend said to him, playing in the same clubs in eastern Germany time and again, dealing with the same promoters, eventually it became an embarrassment to him. They knew how long he'd been here. It ultimately became a question of respect. 'Learning the language is a big step in admitting to yourself that maybe you're here a little more permanently,' says Rasse.

The Wednesday man

If you had to specify a moment in the noughties when it first became clear how much the low-cost airlines and the cheap Berlin rents were changing the city's night life, how international the Berlin scene had become in such a short time, then it could be the 'M' parties held at the WMF summer location from 2004. The venue was a very large, attractive club close to Jannowitzbrücke S-Bahn station. Half of it was in the rooms of a disused office building, the other half was outside in the courtyard. The 'M' stood for '**Mittwoch**', because the parties were always held on a Wednesday, the first Wednesday of the month – and if you turned the flyer upside down, the 'W' stood for 'Wednesday'. The flyers were somewhat mysterious, because apart from the 'M' and the address of the club, there wasn't much on them. The man behind the party was Dave Turov, and the cheap and cheerful entry price, in spite of the numerous big-name DJs on the line-up, was not the only thing that made it unique. It was also the fact that there were hardly any Germans there. Instead, it was teeming with DJs, producers and other people in the music business from all over the world. This was the gathering place for the Brits, the Americans and other internationals who had just moved to the city and wanted to party together.

We meet in Turov's studio in Kreuzberg. There's a drum kit set up in here and some other music production equipment knocking around. Dave Turov is in his early thirties, has black hair and a five-day beard, and radiates that mixture of humour and pragmatic enthusiasm which is shared by many Americans in Berlin.

Dave Turov arrived in 2003 with a rucksack and seventy records which, he recalls, were far too hard – not what he needed in order to make it as a DJ in Berlin. It was music which, at this point, represented how Turov imagined the Berlin techno sound. He had learned to love it from afar. The Berlin clubs had been playing quite different music for a while. At this point, hardly anyone played hard, fast techno any more. Minimal was just beginning its reign over the Berlin dance floors.

As for Turov, he already had several careers under his belt when he moved over. He had earned heaps of money as a consultant for Wall-Street-listed firms. Then the dotcom bubble burst, and he lost his job. For a while he got by as a musician in New York. He played drums in a band, appeared on MTV, organised techno parties in Manhattan. But the techno scene in New York was getting smaller and smaller, and eventually he packed his bags and came to Berlin. 'All the promoters in New York were fighting for the same 100 people, so I took off to where a market existed. It was a combination of wanting to do music seriously and wanting to be in Europe.'

Turov's family comes from Uzbekistan; they were able to leave the Soviet Union at the end of the seventies. His parents were horrified, Turov says, when they heard that he wanted to go to Berlin. They had moved as far west as they possibly could, and now their son was moving back east, of all places. Not only that, but he was moving to Germany. The Turovs are Jewish. 'My mother's father was killed in the war. My grandmother was pregnant with my father in a train going from the Ukraine to Uzbekistan. She told me all these stories about bomb raids and having to flee. We lost a lot of relatives. It's not easy to forgive. My father grew up in a famine. They're a generation for whom history means a lot.'

Turov arrived in a Berlin which appealed to him, but which he had imagined differently, more Russian somehow. 'Maybe I just arrived too late for that.' He began DJing, worked in clubs, including one stint as a glass collector. 'It was quite an experience for someone who had recently been flown around the world as a consultant, paid a six-figure salary and put up in five-star hotels.' He tried to learn German, got a job with the music software firm Native Instruments. But that only lasted a couple of months, and then he began organising the M parties.

A party on a Wednesday was unusual at this point. You could say that it was this party that plugged the last hole between the start of the weekend on a Thursday and the end of the after-party late on a Monday. Turov himself was inspired by his experiences in New York. 'Mondays and Tuesdays in New York are the big nights to go out. For one thing, there are no tourists in town. But more importantly, the people who work in the scene have Mondays and Tuesdays off. The theatres are closed too, so the people who work there can go out as well. It was kind of the same thing here. I was friends with all these people, so the one thing I did successfully was network. We tried not to be so selective at the door; we let anyone in as far as possible. We wanted to make it a party for everybody: black, white, gay, straight, tourists, locals, everybody. Because the best parties are always the mixed parties.' And that's how it was. When the WMF summer location closed, Turov switched to Watergate. The party carried on there for almost three years. Nowadays he holds the party in Weekend. Meanwhile, his idea of organising a party on a Wednesday has prevailed. Just like in New York really, except that – thanks to the low-cost airlines – there's a larger proportion of tourists.

Now Dave Turov has withdrawn a little from the scene. For a while he was always out and about in the city, nurturing contacts, inviting people to his night, distributing flyers, hanging around in record shops. Now he's still organising parties, DJing and making music, but he also studies at the Berlin School of Economics. He wants to stay in Berlin, even though he has lost many of his original illusions about the city.

'You need much less money to get by in Berlin than in other cities. That's why so many painters, designers and other creatives move here. But that can be a problem too. There are lots of people who think that Berlin is this creative utopia, but it's really not. You have to be very self-disciplined if you want to make something of yourself here. Berlin is a very hard place to be productive. A lot of people don't do anything. They just hang out and relax. They live a way only our generation can do. Only our generation has this luxury of not having to fight for what we need, and with this perspective it was very easy to be lazy. I definitely wasted a lot of time. I bought into this I'm-so-creative-and-whatever-in-Berlin attitude. In New York it's swim or die. You're late for work – you lose your job. Then you can't pay your rent and you're fucked. But here it's easier. If you can't pay your rent, you pay it later, or you move in with a friend because the apartments are so huge that there's enough room for everyone anyway. But this can be a very deceptive freedom. If you're not disciplined, you can easily get lost.'

Please go back to zero, Bang Bang Berlin

This reputation of the eternal underground capital has stuck to Berlin for a good forty years, and the Berlin underground has also been an immigrant culture for about the same period. Whether it's the students and the military service evaders, the autonomous communities and various outsiders living lives of leisure, or the famous Swabians, who first took over Kreuzberg, then Berlin-Mitte – without this constant influx, Berlin would not have developed any pop-cultural appeal at all. The sole exceptions may be the gangsta rappers of recent years, who are mostly Berliners, even though many of their parents are immigrants.

These cultures have always been involved in a constant exchange with the rest of the country – although this used to take place via hitchhiking and lift-sharing rather than flying. In the eighties it was your friends in Kreuzberg that you would go to visit (the last volume of Sven Regener's **Herr Lehmann** trilogy ells a nice story about this); in the nineties many West and East German scene tourists knew people who lived 'in the East'. Many of these visitors then got hooked on Berlin themselves. The same thing applies today, except the process has moved to a European level.

Interestingly, people's ideas of Berlin haven't changed much at all – the same things continue to fascinate those who have just arrived in Berlin, whether they're from Bremen or from Liverpool. Take a flick through **Bang Bang Berlin**, for example, a wonderfully zany English-language magazine brought into existence by the artist Paul Snowden. It's a celebration of Berlin which can probably only be fully appreciated as an Easyjet raver: an expression of wonder, generously sprinkled with exclamation marks, at how cool Berlin is. The only difference nowadays is that the importance of German history is fading more and more into the background – little by little, the last remaining bullet holes in the rearmost courtyards are being plastered over.

However, this ability to start again from zero has itself been part of

Berlin pop culture for a long time, the motto being: everything's ruined here, let's start again from scratch. You can hear the historically motivated break with history in the krautrock experiments of a band like Cluster, who wanted to completely reinvent music in the late sixties, taking electric bleeps as a starting point. Or in the noise experiments of Einstürzende Neubauten in the early eighties. At the start of the techno movement in the early nineties, too, many people had the feeling that the great boom-boom-boom could inject new life into everything again.

For the makers of **Bang Bang Berlin**, Berlin is a blank page to which they can attach any labels they want. They celebrate the techno culture of the noughties, in glorious ignorance, as the 'first cool German pop culture', and continue to pursue the same line that has been peddled time after time by different generations of West and East German immigrants: thinking prefab apartment blocks are a good thing, discovering Friedrichshain, telling everyone how cheap it is in Berlin. Daringly they venture into the suburbs to return with romanticised tales of the superb architecture in Marzahn or Märkisches Viertel. Meanwhile, the whole thing is emblazoned with the logo designed by Snowden which has long-since become a Berlin export in its own right, being paraded across the world on printed t-shirts: 'Wasted German Youth'. People have even been seen wearing it in Buenos Aires.

All of this is possible because Berlin has not been subject to anywhere near the same level of media exposure as the world's other major cities. For several decades the cityscape of Berlin was almost completely ignored while the skylines of London, Paris or New York were reproduced on an industrial scale and made instantly recognisable. The few images of Berlin painted a vague picture in which the wild parties of the twenties merged seamlessly into Nazi marches and the bombed city of 1945. Here there are still things to discover.

The four pillars of Berlin night life: Friday

In front of Tresor is a car park. So what, I hear you say, you have to park somewhere. Sure, people who live in a state which covers a large rural area, like Bavaria or North Rhine-Westphalia, are used to driving to clubs. A Berlin club promoter, on the other hand, has all kinds of things to consider when planning a club, but a car park is not one of them. Most people don't come by car. Either they're tourists and have arrived in the city by plane, or they live relatively near to the club. In both cases, it means they get to the party on public transport, by taxi or by bike. Besides, as everyone knows, you shouldn't get behind the wheel unless you're sober.

Nevertheless, Tresor has a car park. One reason is that it was already there before the club existed – it used to accommodate the cars of the workers from the now decommissioned power station on Köpenicker Straße which is the club's current home. The other reason is that it needs one. Many Tresor clubbers actually do come by car, and this is because of where they live – Tresor is very popular with 'Ossis' (easterners).

This statement needs to be qualified right away: Tresor itself is in former East Berlin. It may be on the border with Kreuzberg, but it's on the east side of the wall's former route. If you live within walking distance, there's a fair chance you're an Ossi yourself and you certainly wouldn't come by car. 'Ossi', in this case, is not meant as the opposite of 'Wessi', but as a term to describe one of the three groups which have been cornerstones of Berlin night life since the nineties: the Ossis, the gays and the creatives, sometimes also called 'Mittis'. In the noughties, they have been joined by a fourth and equally important group: the tourists or 'Touris'.

Of course, this is a very crude classification which often doesn't hold true upon closer inspection. Many gay people come from the East, as do scores of people working in creative industries. There are also gay tourists, of course, just like there are gay creatives. But without such crude classifications, it would be impossible to separate such a fragile social structure as Berlin's night life into groups at all. So it may be an oversimplification, but that doesn't make it completely invalid. For instance, it was the great clubbing allegiance of Ossis and gays that supported the techno scene throughout the early nineties; many of the smaller clubs of the mid-nineties were not only in Berlin-Mitte, they were also frequented by Mittis; and the clubbing scene of the noughties would never have developed such a dynamic if the Easyjet raver had not emerged as a new player on the Berlin stage.

As for Tresor, it would surely not have kept going for so long had it not been for the loyalty of those Ossis who, at the very beginning, used to arrive behind the wheel of a Trabi or a Wartburg.

The new Tresor has managed to transfer a fair portion of its original charm into its new location. From your first step through the door, you have the feeling of being inside an old industrial ruin. Not only because you are indeed inside one, but also because of the smell. Once you're through the entrance, you're surrounded by the comforting smell of damp plaster. Some steps lead up to the so-called Batterieraum, the main room of the new Tresor. The toilets and the cloakroom are down the stairs and to the left, and to the right is a long passageway which leads to the basement dance floor – very much like the old Tresor. Indeed, making your way into the new basement is a little like taking a trip back in time: it's dark, the bass is booming, and as you go round the corner you find yourself standing between the old safety deposit boxes. A couple of lesser-known DJs are belting out some techno of the harder variety. It's techno hell just as you would imagine it – and just like back in the day.

Playing upstairs on this Friday night are resident DJ Suzi Wong and Blake Baxter, a Detroit techno veteran. Baxter was one of the first to make his way over to Berlin, back when he called himself the Prince of Techno. He's been coming back regularly ever since, and has released over a dozen records on the Tresor label. With the poise of an experienced pro he lays down a quality set of percussive Detroit techno. The club is half full, the atmosphere relaxed.

A new sound system was installed in the Batterieraum a few weeks ago. You don't notice it at first because it does away with the usual four large speaker stacks in the corners of the dance floor. Instead there's a ring of around two hundred mini speakers suspended above the dance floor. If a musician has the corresponding software programme, they can now send individual audio objects wandering across the room as they see fit. It changes nothing for the DJs, though; you can't produce these effects using records. Nevertheless, it sounds excellent.

The Batterieraum is a large, oblong room with a dance floor

towards the front and a bar at the back. At the end are some steps which lead outside into the remarkably ugly Tresor garden, another tradition carried over from the old location on Leipziger Straße. At least that one had a couple of trees. This one is completely bare except for concrete walls, a couple of seats and a wire-mesh fence.

I stand at the bar in the Batterieraum. Even in this dim light, you can see that the barwoman with the pierced eyebrow spends a lot of time at the tanning salon. Next to me is a young man; we talk for a moment while waiting for our drinks. He comes from Köpenick, a locality in the south-east of the city, studies environmental technology, and says he comes here regularly. Then I get talking to a young Greek guy who's there with his uncle. He actually feels much more at home in the hip hop scene, he says, but his uncle, a Berlin filmmaker who also DJs from time to time, wanted to take him to a proper techno club before he flies back to Greece. Both of them like it here. They're not exactly sober either. Later I see them standing together on the dance floor, smiling away happily.

There's a complicated set of rules governing a city's night life. No one has ever written them down because they're constantly changing. To keep up with them you just have to carry on going clubbing regularly. One of the eternal, fundamental principles, however, is seniority – originally a method used by the army to organise promotions within the officer corps according to the officers' length of service. Today the principle is only used in the diplomatic corps, where the diplomats' ranking on particular occasions is governed by the age of the letter of credence presented by the host country. But it also applies to night life – **De:Bug** magazine once made a joke of it in a fashion editorial by pinning a selection of club tags to the lapels of various Berlin night-life veterans like medals. This principle partly explains the scene's aversion to tourists – they're only there for a weekend or two.

Behind the resentment between Mittis and Ossis, on the other hand, lies a class conflict. The former tend to be from middle-class families, the latter tend not to be. The Mittis often belong to the 'digital bohemia', a term coined by the journalists Holm Friebe and Sascha Lobo in their book **Wir nennen es Arbeit** (We Call it Work). It refers to people for whom legally and financially precarious working conditions are seen as an opportunity rather than a threat; people who have gained good qualifications and are now working for an agency or as freelancers; people who feed content to the media industry, programme websites or do some other job which they have difficulty describing accurately to their parents. Mittis who are not part of the digital bohemia might be in with the Berlin fashion scene, designing clothes themselves or selling them in one of the countless small boutiques. Sometimes they are still studying at the same time or writing a thesis or doctorate, or they are part of the art scene. In many cases they are also unpaid or low-earning interns who are funded by their parents, and in most cases these parents do not live in Berlin. For the Mittis are generally people who have moved to Berlin, largely from western Germany.

Like all class conflicts, this is reflected in questions of taste: the Mittis regard their musical preferences as more sophisticated, an attitude which is primarily articulated via an urgent thirst for the present. They want to feel like they constantly have their finger on the pulse. This is probably the primary reason why you so seldom come across them in Tresor: the club gives them the impression of a conscious conservatism of techno values which, for them, holds very little appeal.

Clothing also mirrors these different attitudes. The hipster fashions of the noughties have left little trace on the Tresor crowd. No one here is wearing skinny jeans or narrow, low-cut trousers. You don't see any printed t-shirts with long, asymmetrical cuts; there are no coloured glasses, ironic moustaches or braces vying for your attention. The way that this crowd is dressed is closer to a street style: parkas, hoodies, combat pants and baseball caps. Even the good old Underground Resistance sweater is on show, the white 'UR' on a black background, which was an omnipresent badge of identification in Berlin night life of the nineties.

Underground Resistance was and is one of the most important Detroit techno labels; many UR artists also released records on the Tresor label in the nineties. The most famous of them is probably Jeff Mills, who had a very close relationship with Tresor and, for a long time, was globally recognised as the epitome of the techno DJ.

There's also a **Kistenstapelraver** or 'box-stacking raver' in attendance. In the nineties, this is what the Mittis used to call those ravers from the surrounding state of Brandenburg who had a very particular style of dancing: while the rest of their body remained relatively still, except for a pelvic motion, and even their facial expressions had to stay absolutely frozen, they would wave their arms around in front of their face in constantly varying combinations. They looked like robots stacking boxes. And there was a particular outfit to go with it: shoes with platform soles, trousers made from shiny synthetic material with large flares at the bottom, a very tight t-shirt and a short 'bird's nest' haircut, which was shaved at the sides and styled into a nest at the top. It was an outfit which would probably make you just as few friends on the streets of small Brandenburg towns like Schwedt or Oranienburg as it would in Berlin-Mitte. It was an extremely artificial look, a homage to plastic, exaggerated in its colours, its high visibility, and its accentuation of the body. Small town techno glam. At the end of the nineties this was a very prominent subculture within the scene. Today there's just this one guy, and his friends are wearing hoodies. He's dancing in front of the DJ booth.

So far, the question as to why techno has been able to reach such enormous popularity in eastern Germany has not been fully answered. Apart from the area around Frankfurt, there can't be any other region where techno is such an integral part of people's musical socialisation. Yet whereas in Hesse, the federal state of which Frankfurt is the capital, this situation is inextricably linked to the figure of Sven Väth, for eastern Germany it's much more difficult to explain. It certainly has something to do with the fact that techno was the soundtrack to which Germans celebrated their new freedom in the years after the wall came down. But this, according to almost all the DJs and producers who grew up in the East, is not the whole story. Even when the wall was still standing, they were listening to new wave or Depeche Mode – music that exhibited a similar coldness of sound to the techno records which arrived later. Interestingly, this music was also having a certain effect at the same time on those figures in Detroit who were soon to invent techno music and come over to play it in Berlin after the fall of the wall.

Another question which remains open is why so few people with Turkish or Arab parents participate in the Berlin techno scene. The scene is colourful, but then again, not to the point where you see lots of German Turks or German Arabs in the clubs. In Berlin, and all over Europe, hip hop may be the pop culture which offers the most appealing narrative to second- and third-generation migrants. But this is only half the story, as in Frankfurt or Mannheim they are an integral part of the scene. In Berlin they are seldom seen.

One place they come to, however, is Tresor. Two young men with dark hair and hairy chests are dancing with their t-shirts off whilst whistling and cheering for the DJ. Suzi Wong has stepped up to the decks in the Batterieraum. She's mixing raw Chicago house with European techno; the delivery is straight-up and direct. At one point while she's playing there's some noticeable feedback. She hears it, thinks for a second and then builds it into her set. She allows the humming to go on for a couple of seconds, then takes out the bass, the humming fades, then she slams the bass drum back in again. A young man who's stood in front of the DJ booth cheers and shouts 'Techno! Techno!'

After a while I need some fresh air; I leave Tresor and take a walk around the block, up Köpenicker Straße to Heinrich-Heine-Straße U-Bahn station. For many years, this was home to Sage Club, a place which changed styles every day of the week, with Sunday being a techno night. Now this is where Kitkat Club holds its sex parties. The people from Sage, meanwhile, have opened up Rechenzentrum, a very large and attractive club a few kilometres down the Spree, on the site of the former GDR radio broadcasting organisation on Nalepastraße. This building complex has been under renovation for years; there are plans to install music production and recording studios here, and occasional concerts are already being held in the former broadcasting studio. Rechenzentrum is in a neighbouring building which used to be the telephone switchboard. The vision of the people behind the club is not dissimilar to that of Tresor: they want to make a club where the sound is a little techier and which also appeals to people who don't live in one of the central districts. In the summer the club spreads out onto a large beach area on the banks of the Spree. A shuttle boat service is in place to pick people up from a jetty on the other side of the river in Treptower Park. The Rechenzentrum site is also equipped with a large car park.

On the way back I come across two guys and a girl. They're in disagreement as to where the night should go from here. The two guys want to carry on the party in Panoramabar. The girl wants to go home and then go out again tomorrow. I look round to see what the outcome is. They get into two different taxis.

Ricardo

He's the biggest DJ star of the noughties. A portrait of Ricardo Villalobos, who has helped shape the Berlin scene with his epic sets, his radical music and his desire for excess.

There are many stories told about Ricardo Villalobos. They probably outnumber stories about any other DJ of the present time. And though they vary enormously in their details, in essence they always go something like this: went out, got mashed, Ricardo played, was great, then I can't remember exactly but Ricardo was definitely still playing an absolute blinder, then we went to such and such a club, and suddenly Ricardo's there too, he's stood behind the decks playing this quality set, somehow I didn't feel like going home yet, and anyway I'd met what's-his-name there as well, then we went out for a bit and when we came back it was dark again, but Ricardo was still playing. It was wicked. Completely knackered of course but yeah, wicked.

That's how the Ricardo stories go, and they are interesting for two reasons. Firstly, they are stories of a star, if you understand star not as a celebrity, but in the old-fashioned sense of a combination of life and work – a form of existence in which life in the public eye and artistic activity illuminate and intensify one another. Secondly, they are stories of you and your mates; they almost always have room for the role of the narrator. Ricardo Villalobos may be the biggest star to emerge from club culture in the noughties, but his feet always remain firmly on the ground of the club he's playing in. Somehow these stories don't give you the impression that Ricardo Villalobos would like to meet for an interview at ten o'clock on a Wednesday morning. Especially as initially, he wasn't keen on the idea at all. 'Ah come on,' he says on the phone, 'there are already so many articles, just get hold of one of the magazines.' Then the next time we speak, a week later, he agrees almost immediately: 'Oh yeah, the interview. How many hours do you need then? Two? Three?'

We meet at the Ankerklause bar in Berlin-Kreuzberg on a sunny winter's morning. Villalobos lives nearby. Another surprise is how fresh he's looking. Admittedly, he's wearing his large sunglasses, which he keeps on throughout the interview, but otherwise there's nothing that recalls Ricardo the über-raver who has been burned onto the collective conscience of the house nation. Almost nothing. Just that characteristic posture which Villalobos has when he's behind the decks, the way he constantly sways in time with the rhythms, leaning slightly forwards and concentrating intensely as he flicks through his crates of records – he looks a bit like this when he's talking to you, too. Villalobos sways in time to his own words; he basically speaks with his entire body. For him, argumentation is movement. Even excess, we learn, requires discipline. The weekends are for flying round the world and playing records; Tuesday to Thursday is studio time.

It's mid-February 2007. The excitement over his great track 'Fizheuer Zieheuer', a 37-minute-long dub meditation built around a looped sample of the horns from a gypsy orchestra, has yet to fully subside. Another track attributed to Villalobos is continuing to do the weekly rounds: a bootleg remix which strips Depeche Mode's 'The Sinner In Me' down to its bare components. He's currently working on his contribution to the monthly mix CD series of the London superclub Fabric. His CD doesn't function like a normal DJ mix, however. It consists entirely of his own tracks. This is partly to do with Villalobos' great annoyance at the omnipresence of his DJ sets on the internet – recordings of live sets which have, in most cases, been made and released by someone else without his knowledge.

'I couldn't be bothered making a mix CD,' he says. 'Making a mix CD means you want to put together a mix of your favourite music. But often you can't get the music you want. Either you can't get the labels on board or they don't even exist any more. So you don't have complete freedom; you can only use the tracks which are easy to license.' For Villalobos, who is famed for his eclectic track selection, this poses a real problem. 'Besides, there are already so many of my mixes out there, unfortunately. Including some with my own tracks. They're floating around on the internet because someone or other uploaded them. I don't like that. The way I've done this now makes it a bit more special. Plus, I was able to maintain a particular conception of how the sound should be. That said, it still sounds like a DJ mix.'

Released in September 2007, **Fabric 36** turned out to be a brilliant album: minimal house music full of warmth, bleeps and bloops of the highest order. Sometimes it goes off on a tangent, only to find its way back to the kick drum again. It's an album full of surprising ideas. It's simmered down to the essentials and nevertheless laden with crude nonsense and great pathos – all those things so often missing in a music business that's taken so deadly seriously. You could say it's a record like a party. A good half of the tracks are collaborations with other artists, most of which came about because the collaborators happened to stop by at Villalobos' studio.

But the most astonishing thing about his music – especially as it comes from a star DJ – is how fundamentally radical it is, how uncompromisingly Villalobos pursues his artistic intentions as a producer. If things were to take their normal course, he would complement his flourishing DJ career, which has taken him from small dance floors to superclubs, with productions designed to increase his own prominence as a DJ. But he has taken the opposite route. That's not to say he hasn't had any hits: '808 Bassqueen' from 1999 was one, so were 'Easy Lee' and 'Dexter' from his **Alcachofa** album, his Depeche Mode remix, certainly, and anyone who's seen the YouTube video of the two Spanish twelve-year-olds hopping around their room to 'Fizheuer Zieheuer' knows that this marathon monster jam has its hit properties too. Yet these are the exceptions. Since the success of **Alcachofa**, Villalobos' records have become increasingly idiosyncratic. Take the 2005 album **Thé Au Harem D'Archimède**, which was created from the ruins of a KLF remix which just wouldn't work out: a polyrhythmic, meditative blend of sparkles and twinkles. Or **Achso** from 2006: four long pieces which, if you were to take away the beats, sound closest to a certain variety of cool European jazz sketches. Indeed, there are stacks of CDs from the ECM label lying around Villalobos' studio, and on a shelf on the wall are jazz albums from every possible period and genre.

From samba to rave

Ricardo Villalobos was born in Chile in 1970. After the coup d'état against the socialist government of Salvador Allende in 1973 his family, like thousands of others, had to leave the country, and they ended up in the West German city of Darmstadt. Villalobos' musical socialisation can be regarded as a dual process. On one hand, his parents' house was full of other exiled Chileans who listened to and made music together. He also travelled to South America regularly from the mid-eighties onwards. He took percussion lessons, was introduced to the world of Afro-Cuban and Afro-Brazilian rhythms while staying in Cuba and Brazil, and once his father took him along to a samba school festival in Rio de Janeiro which went on for several days. On the other hand, in the early nineties he began hanging around the clubs in the party city of Frankfurt, and eventually started putting on his own nights. There are some lovely stories about Villalobos' early DJ years: Carl Craig apparently once played for nine hours in his parents' basement, and Villalobos is said to have bought his first equipment with the money he made from flogging his collection of Depeche Mode records.

That basically sums up the influences which have made Ricardo Villalobos into such an extraordinary figure. You might call his particular approach an open interpretation of rave culture based on a South American understanding of rhythm. Or, you might say, a conception of music which favours the loop, continuity, getting lost in the groove; one which doesn't rely on anthems or direct hits of euphoria; one which aims towards the promised land of house, towards making the dance floor into a utopian space, and (Villalobos emphasises the importance of this time and again) towards having club music understood as a shared activity, as a bond of friendship.

There's one more ingredient to be added: Berlin. In fact, Villalobos' arrival in the city coincided with a revolution so dramatic that it now goes unnoticed, so deeply have its consequences become ingrained into the daily lives of those involved in the scene: the rise of after-party culture reshaped Berlin's clubbing life, paving the way for its current global fame.

Yes, people went clubbing and stayed out for a long time in the eighties and nineties, too. Illegal and semi-legal clubs have always been around as well. But when the legendary techno club Ostgut had to shut in 2002, something interesting happened. Deprived of their focal point, many of the city's roaming hedonists began to regard the time before Sunday morning purely as a transitory period, a warm-up phase of sorts, which served the purpose of getting ready for the most important part of the weekend, the after-party. Previously these parties were meant to help you come down gently after a night of partying. Now they became the main event.

Ricardo Villalobos and his friends elevated after-party music to an art form all of its own. In Maja Classen's documentary film **Feiern**, DJ and producer Ewan Pearson derisively remarks that after a certain hour in Berlin, people would carry on dancing even if you just stood there banging a wooden spoon on a saucepan – and this is actually a fairly accurate description of Ricardo Villalobos' basic method. Using simple percussive loops as a foundation, he constructs a musical landscape which spreads in every direction, taking the liberty of sprawling outwards in time and space without the need for an anchor, just like the people following the groove on the dance floor. Some of the consequences are surprising. It may be that this music complements the post-euphoric high of certain drugs particularly well, but considering its twistedness, its popularity is nevertheless astounding.

Listening to Villalobos' music is a matter of learning patience, and this is something which comes easier on a dance floor at one o'clock on a Sunday afternoon, when simple concepts of linear time have left you and time is able to stretch and shift, bend and undulate, than it does on a Tuesday morning on your way to work. The peak time is behind you; you no longer feel the need to be driven along by the heavy thump of the kick drum; you're open to other rhythmic patterns. These are the moments described in most Villalobos tracks.

Much as he distrusts any form of hype, the popularity of his sound can be traced back in large measure to his personality and to the quite unique connection he's able to establish with a dance floor. 'Well, a crowd is like a soup,' he says when asked what he pays attention to while playing. 'At Club der Visionäre, for example, you've got the girls who are into house at the back in the corner, and they always go to get a drink if I play a techier track. So I try to play something which will keep them on the dance floor, but which also appeals to the guys who are into techno – you know, the clenched fists and 'bring it on' crowd. And then you have your own vision of what it is that makes people dance, too. The truth about this dance floor, what is that? Given these circumstances, what will make an impression on these people here? How deep does the bass have to be? What's the right frequency? How does the kick drum have to be? How do the individual percussive elements have to fit together to make it groove? When should the melody come in? When should something come in to take people in another direction entirely – and then rein them back in again? These are the experiences you have on the dance floor. That's also why it's so important for all DJs to produce music as well. Music has to be driven forward. DJing is a thing of the present. Production is a snapshot of the future. It's what moves us forward.'

The dream of the ideal club

You can have long discussions with Villalobos about what moves us forward. In terms of music, for instance, he's far from content with the horizons he has explored so far. Just a question about whether he'd also been to northern Brazil during his travels in South America provokes great enthusiasm: unfortunately he hasn't, he says, but what about the unbelievable time signatures they use over there! Or on a social topic: along with several other producers he has founded the Narod Niki project, a laptop orchestra which performs at irregular intervals. It's a minimal house super-group which tries to avoid being precisely this. Although famous producers such as Carl Craig, Luciano, Robert Henke and Moritz von Oswald are involved, as a rule they don't announce in advance who will be participating in a particular concert. The performances themselves are long jam sessions of music constantly morphing from one form to another.

In view of the restrictions currently faced by clubs – the smoking ban, which is having an effect on everyone, strict door checks, occasional raids – Villalobos is also keen to talk about his idea for a club of the future, about the way the speakers would have to be set up there and, with equal enthusiasm, about how this club couldn't be focused on making money. He describes the dance floor, which he regards as 'a gathering in its most democratic form', as follows: 'There are no stars, people get each other drinks, everyone talks with one another, everyone dances with one other. Everyone's dancing for the same reason. Yes, you have to charge a small entry fee to pay for the sound system, but it's essentially an anarchistic situation. It's like air molecules which disperse themselves around a room. The capitalist system would like to gather all these air molecules together in one corner and then sell them. But actually things should be different: everyone should get what they need – in every corner of the room. But the way our world works is all wrong. Here, all the molecules are gathered together in one corner, and everyone else has to think about how to get over there. So that they can breathe. Those that don't make it are left for dead. And if you preach exactly the opposite then it soon becomes clear that restrictions will come, that this is not approved of. That's why it's important not to be political, but to define yourself as political.'

Villalobos is a political person. Due to the role played by the CIA in the coup d'état against Allende, and because he was treated as a suspicious person by border officials when entering the USA, he refuses to play in the states. When interviewed, he never tires of condemning the shady setting in which decisions over war and peace are made, decisions which the rest of the world never hears about, although it has to live with the consequences.

You could paint this outlook as the source of the 'dark energy' running through Villalobos' productions, as the American critic

Philip Sherburne did in **The Wire** magazine. But there is a more interesting angle. If you combine 'not being political, but defining yourself as political' with the experience of time unique to Villalobos' productions and DJ sets – making them so all-embracing, so 'I don't want to go home yet' – then you arrive at a political model not so far removed from ideas prevalent in other areas of pop culture.

Didn't Tocotronic make an extremely eloquent appeal to 'surrender' on their album **Kapitulation**? Have our lives not been haunted in so many respects by Bartleby the scrivener from Melville's eponymous story, with his famous refrain, 'I would prefer not to'? Isn't the idea of exodus a central theme when Hardt and Negri sketch out their politics of multitude? This is what it boils down to. It's not a simple matter, but these things have never been simple.

Berghain, the centre of the world
by Alexis Waltz

Berghain towers like a techno cathedral on the fringe of the new club mile. It stands not only for an uncompromising vision of clubbing, but also for a sound which could only have been created here.

A cold spotlight shines down on the mass of people waiting to be let into the box-shaped structure. You hear conversations in all kinds of languages and look into the disappointed faces of those turned away at the door. Jeans pockets, purses and wallets are thoroughly searched. The Berghain feeling sets in as soon as you get to the cloakroom. You pass through the labyrinth of concrete pillars which supports the dance floor, and as you climb the steps your view opens out to reveal the techno cathedral. A shiver runs through you. Only shadows reveal the contours of the room. The mighty concrete of the former generator room radiates the raw, industrial energy of a past era. You look out onto the dance floor: on the right the blue light of the bar shines through the large glass windows, on the left another staircase leads up to Panoramabar. You could never grow used to this space to the point where it appears normal, and this means it can become a setting for unimaginable pleasures.

For the first few hours there's a sense of innocence and curiosity about the night. The Berghain dance floor is not really crowded; there's no nervous bustle, nothing to distract you from listening to the music and dancing. A primal groove emanates from the speakers; a raw pulse creates a focused, hypnotic foundation which is pierced by occasional moments of euphoria. These sounds are created by Marcel Dettmann, one of the resident DJs who shape the club's musical direction. The use of drum patterns is central to his music, structuring his sets by shifting simple rhythms and sparse sounds. His angular face has an air of concentration and resolve as he mixes. Occasionally there are moments when he soaks up the party feeling and the music and has a little dance. Sometimes a sense of profound pleasure is visible on his face. He's casual and committed, relaxed and excited, all in absolutely equal measure. There's no trace of melody in the basslines; the sounds which emerge are isolated and detached. Short, incisive figures. The raw, dirty, sketch-like quality of the music produces a special kind of spontaneity and suspense. The set could be compared to a Buddhist ritual serving to peel away the sentimentality and nostalgia of the pop music which surrounds us in everyday life.

Techno can be this sexy

The Berlin club scene in 2009 has two poles: at one end the parties are about fashion, alcohol and socialising; at the other end everything revolves around drugs. When music is at the centre of things, the events often seem stilted and nerdy. But wherever your preferences lie, in every scene, Berghain and Panoramabar stand for emphatic, all-out clubbing. The club's unique status is born out of its integrative nature. Instead of orienting itself towards a particular segment of society, it allows every individual party-goer to measure how far they can push their limits of excess. Berghain is flawless: whereas the interior design of a club often reflects the vanity of those who run it, here, in this former power plant, only the strictly necessary changes and installations have been carried out.

The distinction between Berghain and Panoramabar reflects the dualism of techno and house which structures electronic dance music. The style of music in the club's predecessor Ostgut, which existed from 1998 to 2003, was no-nonsense techno. Panoramabar, added later as an extension, was innovative in its musical style. A very particular sound evolved here, ranging between elegant minimal and timeless, uplifting house.

This is still the case today, except now the techno room at Berghain is also developing its own unique direction. Since Berghain opened in December 2004, its resident DJs André Galluzzi, Len Faki, Marcel Fengler, Marcel Dettmann, Norman Nodge, Fiedel and Ben Klock have invented a novel and distinctive techno sound. The volume of the room, the intensity of the bass, the ultra-clear Funktion One sound system, the loyal crowd and particularly the long sets of up to eight hours have provided the DJs with a unique performance situation. Hardly any large clubs grant their residents such a platform for experimentation. 'My sets have changed a lot as a result of their length,' explains Len Faki. 'Interaction with the crowd reaches another level. At Berghain, at the point where the peak-time DJ would normally be finishing, you're just getting started. You have to give 100 percent and you get 200 percent in return.'

The DJs all arrived at the club with a particular understanding of techno developed over a period of years. In the laboratory situation of the Berghain dance floor, a sound has been created which takes the volume and energy from hard techno, but decreases its tempo in order to bring about a new, meditative depth. 'The slower tempo wasn't a conscious decision,' says Ben Klock, 'techno records from the nineties get this sexiness when you pitch them down by six or eight percent.' Whereas André Galluzzi, with his dark techno sound, rolling basslines and charismatic presence, was the DJ who most heavily influenced the style of the old Ostgut, the current Berghain residents complement one another. Marcel Dettmann, for instance, loves to play a rugged, bleak kind of techno and cultivates an analytical method of working with sounds; in Len Faki's more opulent style there are rave-like moments; with Ben Klock you can often detect moments of subtle, underground house music.

A little excursion into the past: Ostgut, where it all began

Berghain's predecessor club was situated slightly to the south, on the other side of the huge area of train tracks between Warschauer Straße and Ostbahnhof – right where O2 World, a huge multipurpose arena, opened in September 2008. Ostgut is the legendary birthplace of noughties club culture. This is where today's dominant clubbing model was developed – this special social constellation in which all party-goers come together under the hegemony of Berlin's gay community. This is a situation where the populism of the large dance floor isn't at odds with the authenticity of the music, as this authenticity is based on a musical experience, not on a desire to isolate oneself from other groups. The old Panoramabar, in particular, was where the current club sound evolved, where techno and house, the new minimal sound and older styles were merged.

It all began while Berlin was suffering from its hangover of the late nineties, when the city's clubs had entered a crisis. All the predominant styles of clubbing music were losing their appeal. The classic, Detroit-bound techno played by someone like DJ Rok was gradually losing its effectiveness on the dance floor. The same could be said of the prevalent American house sound favoured by DJs like Mitja Prinz. The sound of DJ Highfish, successfully exported around the world as Electroclash around the turn of the century, did bring pop back to the dance floor. But in techno-dominated Berlin, rather than generating collective delirium, this new trend led to a fragmentation of the crowd. In social terms, too, the scene was paralysed. On one hand was the generally more stylish, elitist class of Mitte hipsters, and on the other was the underclass of ravers from the surrounding state of Brandenburg. The glamour of E-Werk and WMF had lost its invigorating power, as had the techno authenticity of Tresor.

It was at this time that Michael Teufele and Norbert Thormann opened Ostgut. At first, the gay crowd of the neighbouring sex club partied there on their own to hard, tastefully selected techno music. One half of the dance floor was populated by men with stacks of muscles, shaved heads and bare chests, wearing combat shorts and combat boots, while the rest of the crowd was more diverse, although equally gay. It took some time before word of the club's existence got around in the straight clubbing scene.

For both crowds, the club was a completely new experience. Up to that point, the music at gay nights had remained largely disconnected from the international developments of dance music. And for the straight crowd, the gay scene's insistence on clubbing as one of life's essentials was extremely inspiring. It was as if the weariness which had settled over the parties in the established clubs had been blown away. Older visitors to Ostgut were reminded of their first contact with this music in the early nineties, while the younger crowd was fascinated by its social authenticity: no one came here to boast about it in the agency where they worked the next morning. All that mattered was what was happening in the here and now, and this quickly became legendary.

In January 2003 Ostgut had to yield to the advancing development plans. Its successor, Berghain, opened in autumn 2004, and immediately topped every other club in the city with its combination of a perfect location, stripped-back interior, optimal sound, reliable bookings and flawless service. This time, Teufele and Thormann wanted to make an artistic statement beyond DJ bookings: large photos by Wolfgang Tillmans are displayed on the walls of Panoramabar, concerts at the venue often go well beyond the scope of club music, and the club has founded its own label, Ostgut Ton.

For resident DJs Len Faki, Ben Klock, Marcel Dettmann and Marcel Fengler, the incomparable situation of DJing at Berghain gave a particular stimulus to their productions. As distinct as the individual musicians are, taken together, their records of the past two years constitute one of the most original new blueprints for techno. Nick Höppner, one of the managers of Ostgut Ton, says, 'The tracks show that this is about doing our own thing. No one can be accused of latching on to something which already exists somewhere else.'

This music has been created from an awareness of the experience of the nineties, but it's anything but nostalgic; it doesn't long for years gone by. With its bleakness and reduced tempo it absorbs aspects of the club music of past years, but at the same time it unleashes a rawness and vitality which makes it virtually impossible to imagine as the product of any other club. 'There's a high degree of identification with the club among the core artists,' says Höppner. 'It's inevitable that the sound evolves via the space. The records are tested here, played here; the club is the reference.'

Eastside killer, Westside killer

The example of Marcel Dettmann and Ben Klock, who represent two contrasting Berlin techno biographies, illustrates how the Berghain residents have found a natural path to one another from various backgrounds. Born in 1971, Klock is a child of nineties dance music just like Dettmann, born in 1977. But whereas Klock, a trained jazz pianist and songwriter from the West Berlin borough of Schöneberg, developed his understanding of house and techno in the clubs of Berlin-Mitte, Dettmann got his musical education in the very specific techno culture of eastern Germany.

Marcel Dettmann grew up in an area of prefab housing in Fürstenwalde, fifty kilometres away from Berlin. Before the wall came down, he was a fan of Depeche Mode: 'In the GDR, music was an escape, a way of getting out for a while. Nowadays people have yoga.' In 1992, techno arrived in Fürstenwalde. Its combination of futurism and rebellion against all previously known forms of music aroused a fascination which still grips him to this day. The first Jeff Mills records which Dettmann heard, at the age of sixteen, were mind-blowing: 'It was as if I'd been transported into the future. It was the best film you'll never see. Of course, today you have a completely different perception of this music.'

At the age of sixteen, instead of buying himself a moped, Dettmann got a pair of decks. He played at parties he organised himself in Dresden or Frankfurt an der Oder. At some point a friend gave a cassette of his to the people at Ostgut. Teufele rang him up a few days afterwards, and half a year later he had his residency. Since his teenage years, Dettmann has known that music is his life's mission. He quit his training in retail sales and in 1996 he began running a small record business from home. Later he worked in a record shop and at a distributor, and in 2004 he joined the techno institution Hardwax. Marcel only started producing music in 2006. He has a very clear idea of what techno is for him: 'The kick drum of a track is the reflection of the artist. For me, techno is loops. But it's only when I can listen to a loop for five or six hours that I record it. If a melody has to come in five minutes into a track then the sound is crap. If that's the case, I start something new or I go to sleep.'

Back in Berghain, another night. The party is in full swing; bodies and minds are deeply emerged in the music. Ben Klock appears more composed behind the decks than Dettmann. In moments of high tension he moves his head to the rhythm of the track. He shares Dettmann's principle of roughness, but the tracks are less brittle; often a melody can be heard murmuring somewhere; his stylistic spectrum seems to be larger. His transitions between records are often absorbing. He brings out the tension between the individual tracks very precisely: either the new record intensifies the dynamic of the previous track, or it breaks from it. He was once given the compliment that even boring records sound exciting when he's playing.

The character of the individual record is determined by the context in which it appears. Ben Klock's compositional approach to

DJing can be traced back to his formal musical training. He understood, when practising for hours on end on the grand piano at Berlin University of the Arts, that it's more important for him to place individual elements in contexts than it is to completely master an instrument.

Techno didn't take off in Berlin-Schöneberg like it did in Fürstenwalde: 'A lot of people thought techno was blunt and primitive,' says Ben. 'For me, though, the nineties signified the emergence of something new. The eighties stood for pop, for a superficial kind of music. I thought it was great that things were getting down to the core, that music was becoming more intense and physical, that particular sounds were being brought out. I never understood bands like the Pet Shop Boys.' The 'Macht der Nacht' ('Power of the Night') parties with Kid Paul in the late eighties were a formative experience for him. Later he gained a career foothold as a graphic designer and skipped a couple of years of Berlin club culture. It was jungle that rekindled his interest in dance music, but he soon found a greater intensity in the straight-up club sound of E-Werk, Tresor and WMF. In 1994 he started playing house at Delicious Doughnuts: 'Back then my sets were mellow. They grew more and more forceful over time. This is a direction which has led all the way to Berghain.' Ben's house sound was never playful or song-heavy, which is why he came up against some barriers in Mitte clubs such as WMF and Cookies: 'At some point the music became too blunt and monotonous for the crowd.' After the electroclash wave swept through he was rarely motivated to DJ any more – until his Berghain residency. 'The architecture, the sound: this is exactly how the music is intended. Finally the jigsaw fit together. The first time I played Berghain I took a lot of records with me that I couldn't play anywhere else; in there every single one of them worked. When I'm producing music or buying records I think in the categories Berghain/Panoramabar. The club is the centre and the source of inspiration.' Unlike Dettmann, Klock has been releasing records since the late nineties. In the ingredients that go into his tracks, you can often detect an organic, musical moment bursting forth from the compelling grooves. His compositions always test the limits of tension between individual elements.

When talking to the pair about new records, they precisely identify the exciting aspects of the pieces – or the moments where the tracks drop their guard. With these comments they reveal a deep, sophisticated understanding of dance music which they both share. It's always a matter of bringing out certain essential artistic elements of techno in the changing trends of sound. They have a common preference for tracks which have a sketch-like, punk feel and leave the DJ plenty of creative leeway. Both of them are wary of tendencies to overproduce tracks, to use song-like arrangements, or to create minimal click symphonies. Just as Marcel rejects any moment of trance euphoria, Ben turns away from any meticulously structured house sound using typical timbres. Despite the common ground which exists between them, there are also contrasts: whereas Dettmann subscribes to an analytical school of techno, Ben's sound has traces of Afro-American funkiness. In the case of 'Scenario', a tracked they produced together, Ben wanted to use the version with the melody, Dettmann the one without. In the end, they were both released.

After techno comes more techno

In the same way as ravers are unable to repeat the experience of a night in Berghain anywhere else, DJing there is also different to playing sets in other clubs, which are often much shorter. 'You fly around the world and the parties are always okay,' says Marcel Dettmann, 'but playing in Berghain once a month is important for me. It's my personal play area where I can do whatever I want. It allows me to develop.'

Berghain challenges you in your very existence: it's not only a place to let off steam after your working week, to find a partner or to hear interesting music. It's a free space – what you do there doesn't have to be consistent with your lifestyle outside. Since the club shows you the greatest pleasures imaginable, you have to ask yourself the question: What do I want? Where do I place myself on the map of social, sexual and musical pleasure? Berghain is a place where you learn to look your own desires in the eye.

The artists and promoters of Berghain exude such assurance and composure because they have been through this process themselves. Michael Teufele also emphasises taking a human approach to artistic decisions. He says it's about giving the artists freedom and, if necessary, backing them up. No matter who you speak to, time and again the conversation turns to how at ease all musicians feel in Berghain, how the label came about almost by accident, and how important Teufele's artistic and social intuition is. He ties up the loose ends. Or, in Ben Klock's words, 'There's a certain magic in all the things that Michael brings together.'

In the case of Berghain and Ostgut Ton, the club and the label form an alliance which has no precedents in techno history. Of course, there are often interdependencies: as the hard trance sound of the Harthouse label accompanied many parties in Frankfurt's Omen club, today many releases on Cocoon Recordings embody the noble modernity of the eponymous club. Yet these are better described as parallel developments which resulted from DJs and producers inspiring one another. The nucleus of a style is created somewhere and then it really takes off in a certain club. In contrast, there was no evidence of the sound of Berghain and Ostgut Ton to be found outside of the club. The independence of this cell is what drives its development. All the producers on the label are also DJs at the club. Len Faki says, 'There's something growing here which is still in its infancy.' Dettmann: 'It's the complete package. If I go clubbing just for pleasure, I go to Berghain.'

Queuing, going to Berghain, never wanting to go home: Saturday

Incidentally, when exactly is Saturday? Almost all clubs open at midnight, so a clubbing Saturday is always Sunday already. The time before the clubs open needs filling – in bars, on the street if you really have to, or at home. If you go to a club before one o'clock on a Saturday night, you inevitably end up on an empty dance floor, a dance floor being played to by a DJ who knows full well no one wants to dance at this hour, and who therefore plays music that no one would dance to, if there was anyone there. But there isn't. The people are outside. In the queue.

This is the case everywhere, but especially at Berghain. The queue snakes a long and orderly path over the sandy ground. Bordered at the very back by construction site fencing, then corralled into an S-shape by steel barriers near the door, it's as if these people are queuing to get into another country. And in a sense, they are. A common assumption is that the time spent waiting outside the door of a club has something to do with the exclusivity that the club in question claims to possess. This belief is probably a distant echo of the anguished groans of all those who, at some point in the late seventies, waited to be let into Studio 54 in

New York, the most famous discotheque of the twentieth century. Here, the doorman's reign of terror created that mixture of celebrity, money, beauty and youth to which some still aspire today. You were beckoned to come inside – or not, in which case you just had to stand there and watch. This could go on all night. There was no one forcing you to persevere except for the sheer appeal of gaining some ground in the attention economy which governs the night life of cities where fame, wealth and taste belong together. Berlin isn't one of those cities.

Indeed, all attempts by club promoters in the nineties to open a discotheque that followed this principle ended in fiasco. Taste and money just don't belong together in Berlin, except in the art scene. However, since the nineties this scene has almost entirely given up its once close alliance with the techno and house clubs, along with the idea that every exhibition opening absolutely must have a DJ. Nowadays artists, gallery owners, art collectors and critics prefer to gather in their own restaurants and bars in Berlin-Mitte. This district is also home to the only club where the door policy remotely recalls the principle of Studio 54: Cookies on Unter den Linden.

All these things may run through your mind as you stand in the famous queue outside Berghain. The first and most important difference between this and all other queues is that it's for everyone. There is a guestlist here, too, but it's relatively short and carries no symbolic weight. If you're on it, you still have to wait, you just don't have to pay. Only the night's DJs and their entourage can amble past the queue, plus a few people who have a particular connection with Berghain. This has little effect on the queue, however. Perhaps three or four small groups walk past you in the space of an hour, no more. You can watch them while you wait. It always takes a while, whether it's one, three or six o'clock in the morning. Sometimes there's an extra doorman who stands about halfway up the queue and whose sole responsibility is to send back any wannabees who think, for whatever reason, that all are equal before the door to Berghain – except for them.

In its implementation, this policy actually gives a faint sense of Jacobin Terror. Whether you're a queen or a farmer, it really can happen to anyone. Firstly, then, this door is radically democratic. Secondly, however, it exhibits a refreshing arbitrariness which makes you ask yourself the question each and every time, even after years of getting in without a problem: Will I get turned away tonight?

The queues at most clubs function according to the model of social corruption: everyone has to wait, except for those who know someone who knows someone who can put them on the guestlist. On the one hand, this is the sole advantage that the locals have over the great number of tourists. On the other hand, it's the logical result of life in a city where the most important capital to possess is not financial or cultural, but social.

At the old WMF, the archetypal Mitte club of the later nineties, this led for a while to a system of two entrances: one for the people on the guestlist, and one for everyone else. The queue for the guestlist entrance was often significantly longer than the one for the paying guests. This is partly because a techno club is comparable to a 'club' in the sense of an association. Clubs thrive on being able to nurture this sense of belonging. Being on the guest list is an indication for you and for everyone else of your membership, and this is much more important than not having to pay to get in. After all, the entrance fee is negligible compared with what you spend on taxis, alcohol and drugs over the course of a whole night.

For a while, the promoters of WMF tried to counter this escalation in guest-list hassle by giving out more club tags. If you could get your hands on one, all you had to do was hold it up at the door, say your number so it could be crossed off the list, and you were in. This only provided temporary relief, however, as there were soon hundreds of these metal tags in circulation, and people started to lend them to one another, thus leading to even longer queues on the door.

The critical drawback of socially corrupt door policy also became particularly clear at WMF: the more a crowd takes itself for granted as part of a club, the less motivation they need to simply turn up, and therefore the less exciting it is to be there. When the majority of the crowd at the entrance were simply flashing their membership tags and casually heading to the lounge to discuss multimedia projects, WMF actually became plain boring. Among all the posing and career planning, many people forgot what a club is actually there for – namely for dancing and having a great time.

This is what the Berghain queue is intended to prepare you for. And that goes for everyone. Whether it's the couple who keep telling each other off for fidgeting around, or the group of Italians who look as if they've been reading fanzines back home with style tips for Berlin clubs. Their new-rave look comprises huge coloured sunglasses and haircuts nurtured for maximum asymmetry. The girls are wearing purple leggings and poison-green tops, the guys have post-ironic slogans on their T-shirts. One woman is battling her fear of not getting in with an endless and increasingly confusing lecture on her home city of Wuppertal. The two Dutch guys she's befriended in the queue are preventing her monologue from petering out by muttering an occasional 'hm' and 'ah'. Two other guys are making fun of those who aren't let in while warning one another not to laugh too loud, otherwise they might be on the receiving end themselves.

Your fear of the doorman teaches you the respect you need as you approach the Berghain entrance. All the more so since every single time you come, even after several years, he still exudes that daunting authority of the radical lifestyle with his facial tattoos and countless piercings. His name is Sven Marquart, and when he's not standing here he's a photographer. People who know him say he's very nice.

Berghain not only bears a certain architectural resemblance to a cathedral, it's an actual temple of techno. And whether by design or not, waiting in the queue is the first step in an initiation ritual, soon followed by an unmistakable feeling of butterflies in your stomach as you edge towards the door. You watch as people ahead of you get turned away. You try to figure out the criteria. Most of the time it's pretty simple: groups of young men always have a hard time. If on top of that they are tourists, straight or obviously drunk, things get even tougher. But these are just rough guesses. When a punk who doesn't get in shouts out, 'Fuck you, Germany! You're scum! I'm from Vienna!', everyone has a little chuckle.

You don't want to party with just anyone, so no tears are shed for any of those who are turned away. At the same time, the price you pay for exclusivity is the risk of not getting in yourself.

Your identification with the tormentor is mixed with anticipation and fear – a multitude of contradictory feelings come together on the way into Berghain. And that's the way it has to be; it's the first tension to be released as you finally set foot in the club.

The initiation ritual continues with the thorough drug search carried out in the entrance area beside the cash desk: the ritual cleansing. Then you pay your dues, another religious act, to gain passage to the cloakroom, a huge space which contains a few sofas and is dominated by a giant mural painted by the Polish artist Piotr Nathan. It's called **The Rituals of Disappearance**. The lighting reinforces the feeling of an initiation: it's dark outside, dimly lit in the entrance area, bright in the cloakroom. Then, once you've crossed the final threshold and entered the large hall which you could hear booming from outside, it suddenly gets dark again. You cross the hall, climb the large steel stairs, and even if you already know what you've let yourself in for over the hours to come, you still get a sharp shock every time as you stand facing the dance floor and let the music thunder over you. For a few seconds, as your eyes try to adjust to the strobes, you stumble around in semi-blindness. It's a little like a punch in the face – not only do you have to jostle your way through a mass of sweating bodies which have already been there a couple of hours longer than your somewhat more sober self, you also get physically assaulted by the sound waves of the music.

Time for a drink

Berghain and Panoramabar have a total of six bars spread over three floors. One is in the room on the right of Berghain, next to the large dance floor, a space you can imagine as the side aisle of a gothic cathedral. Just as architects of old created a clever interplay of windows and narrow columns to emphasise the direct link with the heavens, here the spotlights are positioned in such a way as to make the ceiling appear even higher than it actually is. Another bar is slightly hidden to the left of the dance floor, near the darkrooms. There's also a staircase here leading up to Panoramabar, which is a little smaller and brighter than Berghain. Upstairs is house and straight, downstairs hard and gay.

This is where the parallel between rave and religion ends. Not because it would be nonsense in principle – on the contrary: in the gay Afro-American scene, house and religion maintain an intimate relationship. Jack, placed by the inventors of house music at the beginning of all existence – 'In the beginning there was Jack/ And Jack had a groove/ And this groove was the beginning of all groove' (Fingers Inc., 'Can You Feel It') – was an average Joe and a dance floor god at the same time, a redeemer, created by transposing the liberation rhetoric of the civil rights movement into gay black subculture. To fit the goals of this scene, the old promise of emancipation was given a new, extended and more specific meaning, and a large helping of pathos was borrowed from the black churches.

However, even in the Chicago of the mid-eighties, going out to a club was still considered a heinous sin. And it's only in German that the area behind the decks is actually called a 'pulpit' (**der Kanzel**) – English sticks to the more matter-of-fact 'booth'. When you look around Panoramabar, there are precisely two things which the place has in common with a church. As in every church, an attempt is made here to institutionalise the desire for transcendental experience – if this is religion then the Panoramabar congregation shares a deep faith. Apart from this, however, nothing connects these clubbers except the deep desire to get well and truly fucked. The second thing is that when Sunday service begins in church, this place is also packed to the rafters with people who've come to hear what the man or woman in the 'pulpit' has to say.

Taking photographs in Berghain isn't allowed, not even on a mobile phone camera. Because many guests don't want to be photographed while they live out their sexual fantasies, says a doorman when asked as to the reason. This may be so, but above all every photo would be a bridge to the outside world, a reminder that the outside exists at all. No club is so successful at sealing itself off from this outside world as Berghain. The sun may already be high in the sky outside – inside you always seem to be shrouded in an early-morning twilight.

Sure, there are people who do things here for which they seek out a dark corner. Everyone who's been here has seen or heard people having sex on the bar. Or on a sofa. Or next to the dance floor. Even though the explicit sex parties have always been held in the adjacent venue 'lab.oratory' (which has nights for every sexual penchant, so long as it's gay in the broadest sense: from 'Yellow Facts' and 'Fausthouse', 'Beard' and 'Slime' through to the biker party 'Spritztour'), Berghain also has two darkrooms of its own. And there are all kinds of stories about people having done this, that and the other while temporarily freed from all inhibitions.

In most cases, however, stories from Berghain are about somebody talking or listening to some ludicrous drivel, or about meeting or getting to know someone who was completely off their face. Then there are the ones about someone going into the toilets with someone else and one of them feeling either incredibly good or not so good afterwards. Often these stories are still funny when it gets to the middle of the week, but sometimes they're sad.

Above all, however, they have an incredible life of their own. Anyone who's been regularly to Ostgut and Berghain over the years knows from personal experience how these stories have given rise to and constantly reinvented the legend of this club. There's this big collective discussion where you subsequently recount the events of the weekend, tell each other what happened to whom, what you saw, what other people told you, and what they in turn had seen and heard about. It's a conversation in which all these stories are constantly being retold, gaining new emphasis, being weighed up, evaluated and explained. You assure one another that you can't carry on like this, although you're secretly looking forward to giving in to temptation again.

These are quite normal clubbing stories really, things you experience in other clubs too – except that elsewhere it's rarely five o'clock on a Sunday afternoon when you find your way back out into the real world. What sets these stories apart is that they are constantly being interwoven into the great Berghain discussion. Like the one about the man who was fisting his partner on the Berghain dance floor and had a centimetre scale tattooed onto his forearm. Or the one about a friend who went to the toilet and came across a woman he'd never met before. She looked at him and said 'Come on, fuck me right now', but he wasn't too keen on the idea, so she landed him a punch which left him with a black eye for days. Or the one about the guy who was in the toilets having a piss when another guy stood next to him, then suddenly cupped his hand in the jet, drank the piss and disappeared again – 'He could have at least asked!'

This is how the Berghain legend comes about, and it's constantly being perpetuated. What's more, the great discussion has extended well beyond the Berlin telephone network. Nights are discussed in newsgroups; Chinese whispers circulate the stories around Stockholm and Milan. A few people in Melbourne have heard them. Then at some point the **New Zealand Herald** is saying that there are techno clubs in Berlin where sex on the dance floor is the most normal thing in the world. At which point a couple more New Zealanders book their flights to Berlin.

When it comes to creating a legend, it's fairly unimportant whether the events really took place or not. It's enough that the stories exist, that they are recounted and passed on.

Berghain isn't Bar 25, anyway. That's a few hundred metres away, as the crow flies, on the banks of the Spree. It too is preceded by a legend of unbridled partying, but the stories from Bar 25 are more extreme and grotesque. Like the one about the girl who was lying on the grass, using her mobile phone as a vibrator and shouting 'Vagina dialogue! Vagina dialogue!' Compared to these stories, life in Berghain is pretty civilized on the whole. Yes, sometimes people fuck in the metal cubby-holes next to the Panoramabar dance floor. But basically the people here know how to behave themselves. Or they ask you first: 'Sorry mate, I'm just gonna have to talk a load of shit to you for a little while, is that okay?'

In which case you're quite happy to put up with it.

Then you walk around, see what's going on over here and over there, have a drink, go to the toilet and look out of a window from the urinals behind Panoramabar at that odd little stream which snakes through the wasteland. You meet all kinds of people, some you know, some you don't. Whilst you're waiting to be served at the bar, a Frenchman in his early twenties explains that he's a techno DJ from Montpellier and that his coming to Berlin was like a Muslim's pilgrimage to Mecca. On the stairway you get talking to a huge, half-naked skinhead who tells you with a smile that there is no other club like this, 'not even in Russia'. At the edge of the dance floor you pick up the thread of a discussion about dub reggae where you left off a few weeks ago.

And then you dance

On a good night, the dance floors of Berghain and Panoramabar are the best in the world. They seem to bring together the best of twenty years of house and techno. The musical expertise of the crowd is incredible, as is their willingness to throw it overboard when required by the rising curve of euphoria. It's not so much the multicultural charm of this mixture of gay and straight, young and old, guys and girls, Berliners and tourists which makes it so unique, but its ability to develop its own particular dynamic. On a dance floor full of hardened Berlin techno veterans, everyone knows what the score is, but sometimes they can lack the necessary enthusiasm when the DJ slams the bass back in after an eight-beat pause. It's just that they've heard this trick a few times already. If you replaced this whole crowd with young, gay Italians who were at Berghain for the first time and really getting their rave on, it probably wouldn't matter what track was playing – they'd go crazy every time. But the combination is wonderful. Nothing can beat a dance floor which has been formed over the years, which knows what to expect from what DJ, and is nevertheless capable of breaking out of these patterns from time to time. After all, the music changes from one month to another as well.

Then at some point you're in such a misty-eyed state that you vigorously affirm the political dimension of electronic dance music. Which lies, you think to yourself, in the way people interact with one another on the dance floor. You have to behave yourself here, find yourself a space, avoid getting in someone else's way. You have to learn these things, they don't just come to you.

When they're lacking, you tend to get these very intense moments of hate. Like when you get shoved aside by one of those little groups who think the shortest route from the door to the bar is across the dance floor. Or when your arm gets burned because the guy next to you thinks he has to both dance and smoke at the same time (unfortunately now you can't even smoke when you're off the dance floor, except for in the somewhat uncomfortable smoking lounge). Or when two guys who lack experience in channelling their uncontrollable urge to move jostle past you and start jacking back and forth. Then they move to another spot to hop around a bit, only then to wander off somewhere entirely different, barging you out of the way again in the process.

These are the times when you would like to introduce the principle of good governance into a club setting: the good dance floor, where everyone knows what they're doing in spite of everything. Where everyone can be as wasted and as spangled as they like, but still show one another respect. Where space is in short supply, but the remaining shred of common sense dictates that those present won't take up more room than is available. Where no half-wit will force his way through the crowd with three drinks in his hands for his mates who are stood talking in the middle of the dance floor.

These are the kinds of things which cross your mind occasionally.

Or when you think, don't I know her from somewhere? Didn't I meet him somewhere recently? In fact, did we not have a conversation? Who's that guy down at the front anyway? Last Saturday he spent the whole time bouncing around in front of the decks, too. Wicked track, amazing. You ask yourself, does it actually get annoying for the DJs when all these mashed-up people shout over to tell them how unbelievably brilliant it is right now? Or are they happy to hear it? Yet another shard of glass stuck in the sole of your shoe. Can't these people put their damn beer bottles down somewhere instead of just dropping them?

Berghain and Panoramabar possess a different level of euphoria to other clubs. The party curve continues to rise steeply well into Sunday afternoon. This is partly due to the charm of the parallel society which exists inside the club. Here they have really managed to shut out the rest of the world. Or better still, to employ it as an effect, as an additional stimulant, a device for adding intensity. When the lighting guy in Panoramabar opens up the roller blinds for a few seconds, for example, letting the sunlight break through, you can physically feel waves of elation washing over the dance floor. People cheer and raise their arms in the air – flirting, of course, with the thought that too much sun could rapidly make this world disappear: like vampires, the crowd would turn to dust.

Berghain has a very mixed crowd. It wasn't always like this. For a long time its predecessor Ostgut was a gay club where straight people remained a small minority, although they were tolerated if they were there to party hard. The opening of Panoramabar changed this, at first just a little, then considerably. If you wanted to know how the politics of sexual identity in Berlin changed in the nineties, you could very well take the example of the relationship between Ostgut and Panoramabar: queer starts to make inroads into the domain of gay, the breach quickly grows larger, and in the end it's no longer clear what's gay and what isn't, except for the actual sexual preference. Somehow, when you look around on a Sunday afternoon in Panoramabar, everyone's a little queer.

And at some point it comes to an end. After all, Berghain is a club and not an after-party location. You go to the cloakroom and hand over your cloakroom tag, which – just one indication of the attention paid to every last detail – is not a ticket with a number, like everywhere else, but a metal tag on a string which you can wear around your neck or tie on somewhere else. Whatever state you might be in at the end of the night, you will definitely get your coat back. They think these things through here. Which is important when no one is in the soundest frame of mind.

Then you stumble out of the door and into the light. You nod goodbye to the doormen – not that you know them, but because you feel in some way indebted to them. Somehow you have to give the night some symbolic closure. You look around, feel the fresh air on your skin, notice how much you've actually been sweating. You hear the faint ringing in your ears mixed with the twittering of the birds, the chatter of people sitting around having another beer, and the soft rattle of the sound system emanating from the building.

Now you can go home. Or stop by at Bar 25 again.

The gentle bliss of the post-euphoric high: Sunday

There's one kind of Sunday, the one where you simply go home the next morning after you've been clubbing and try to get through your hangover with a little decency. You lie in bed, drink water by the litre and hope that you'll gradually sweat out all the alcohol, nicotine and whatever other substances you've consumed over the course of the night. After a few hours the bed is soaking wet, and you smell like a chemical plant. You watch a bit of TV, eat a little something and hope that eventually the dusk will bring you some sleep. You reach for the phone and find out from your friends and fellow clubbers how they've been holding up, when they got home, whether anything else happened, and you assure one another that you're definitely going to take a break from partying for a while. You can do all of this. Especially in winter, when the night never really turns to day anyway, when it's already dark again by the time you wake up and there's no sensible reason to step outside the door in any case. But then there's the other kind of Sunday, the one where you decide not to go home. Where you leave the club when the sun is already up and go on to the next place. That next place is the after-party, and it can go on for some time. Especially in summer.

Indeed, to merely talk about clubs and night life would only be telling half the story of clubbing in Berlin. The other half of the story – the half which has essentially shaped Berlin's reputation as a kind of metropolitan Ibiza on the banks of the Spree – takes place at the numerous and often changing locations where techno is played in the daytime, mostly outdoors, and particularly towards the end of the weekend. Sometimes you need the view of an outsider to appreciate the size and the beauty of it. Techno in Berlin, a friend visiting from the USA once said – it's like reggae in Kingston Town.

It really is incredible how many possibilities there are for setting up a sound system along this stretch of a few kilometres heading out of the city along the Spree from Jannowitzbrücke – often right alongside beach bars and other outdoor locations which have nothing to do with this music. As such, the people who've not been to bed at all mingle with day-trippers, families and other apple juice sippers who've just had lunch and are spending a warm summer's day outside.

At Club der Visionäre, for instance, at the eastern tip of Kreuzberg on Schlesische Straße, a large terrace on one of the small canals which flow into the Spree. Some weekends Club der Visionäre turns into an after-party location which is both loved and dreaded, particularly on a Sunday night into a Monday. The epic sets that Ricardo Villalobos has played here will be talked about for a long time.

In the afternoon everything here looks much more peaceful. A couple of dozen people are sitting round in the sun drinking coffee or beer; many of them are dangling their feet in the water. One man has slid into the canal. He's standing on the bottom with just his head poking out of the water, smoking a joint and talking to his friends. There's some gentle minimal techno clopping along. No one here looks like they've been partying too hard, but who knows – in the summertime, a flushed face and heavy sweating can be due to many things.

The atmosphere is similarly relaxed in the garden of Alte Weberei a little further down the Spree on Alt-Stralau on the river's east bank. Alte Weberei ('old weaving mill') is an old factory building in the no-man's land between the Elsenbrücke bridge and a new residential development near the water which has been under construction for a few years and is gradually approaching completion. The area has a relaxed suburban feel, although it's fairly near to the city centre.

In the garden of Alte Weberei, however, there's nothing to remind you of the bridge to your right or the middle-class enclave to your left. You'd think you were in the middle of a wood. Among the trees, people are lying on towels or sitting at beer tables. Many have piercings or tattoos; most are in their early thirties and alternative in the non-ironic sense.

It's remarkable how house and techno – at least in Berlin – have penetrated into the soundtrack of scenes which a few years ago nurtured bitter prejudices against any kind of music made on machines. They preferred the unprocessed sounds of guitar strings strummed by the human hand. Perhaps it has something to do with the internet, which has done much to free computers from their former image as evil agents of state surveillance. In any case, here at Alte Weberei they're playing dub techno, a style which, with its soft, pulsing bass and the psychedelic undertones of its reverb effects, sounds as if it were invented for this place. A sign has been put up by the swimming pool they've built in the back corner of the garden: 'No Kids, No Drinks, No Sex'. Lying in the pool is a naked woman with several tattoos; next to her are three small children splashing around.

There have been several attempts in Berlin in recent years to offer new options to a clubbing crowd which has got older – options to fit around the careers and kids which are now part of their lives.

Sundays are particularly popular. One party organiser wanted to set up loft parties in Berlin, based on the legendary New York events which were partly responsible for the invention of disco. The loft parties are still running now, and apparently clubbing veterans and their kids party there together under a canopy of balloons. Smoking is not allowed, drugs are frowned upon, and there's no alcohol, just music and fruit juice. It's not as far-fetched as it sounds – in the more spiritually oriented styles of house and disco there's a long tradition of this desire for a healthy oneness of family, earth and the universe. So far it hasn't really taken off in Berlin. Perhaps the cultural DNA of the city's clubbing crowd is simply itching for a bit of aggro. Parties like those in London, where a club advertised a crèche with the lovely slogan 'No more excuses! Bring your fucking kids!' have not yet made an appearance in Berlin either.

Not even on the site of RAW, a former train repair yard by Warschauer Straße S-Bahn station, which is the current anti-capitalist stronghold of Berlin-Friedrichshain. Following the sound of the kick drum you pass by a café, a concrete wall where people are trying a spot of free climbing, and a flea market which has either been picked bare by a swarm of locusts a few minutes ago or was never meant seriously in the first place. And there, in a warehouse with the sun beating down on its roof, are a few anti-globalists dancing to acid techno. Not really much fun, and there aren't very many of them.

Next stop: Oststrand, a beach bar directly opposite O2 World. Through a gap in the Eastside Gallery you reach a small, sandy forecourt. To the left is a beach volleyball court, and to the right is Oststrand. You can already hear the rumbling coming from an area covered by a canopy.

The occasion is a birthday party for André Galuzzi, former resident at Ostgut and one of the great Berlin DJs of the first half of the noughties. There are more big names on the way; Ricardo Villalobos will be here this evening along with a few others; it promises to be a long night. For the moment, however, the site still looks roughly as you imagine the banks of the Spree to be once the MediaSpree investors have completed their project: clean, tidy, and full of sponsorship logos. The dance floor has been built a couple of meters down into the sand, which is a good way of avoiding conflict with the noise-plagued residents on the other side of the river. The canopy keeps out sun and rain, and behind the DJ booth there's a cordoned-off VIP area filled with sofas where some bored people are sitting and looking out at the rest of the party. The music is deathly boring minimal techno. Almost everyone in the crowd could do with spending a day or two away from the gym.

No doubt this will change over the course of the night, once Ricardo and his entourage rock up, plus all those drawn by his name on the line-up. Until that point, however, it's worth taking a detour over to Berghain. When the weather's fine the party carries on in the garden here from midday. Although garden is surely a euphemism. We're talking about a bar with a roof in an open space dominated by concrete slabs. Although the cheerless design may put you off a little at first, you soon begin to appreciate the place. The concrete is excellent for sitting on, particularly around the dance floor where the slabs are arranged in a semi-circle to form a small amphitheatre. Stretched over the dance floor is a camouflage net with the hose of a sprinkler system weaved into it. Just as other DJs might have a dry ice machine, here a fine mist of water droplets can be made to rain onto the dance floor.

Prosumer is playing one of his trademark sets: stripped-down, sex-charged, yearning Chicago house – perfect music. Retro and yet contemporary. Risky, messed up and beautiful. Looking at the crowd, you can see that they have a long night behind them. They're sitting or lying peacefully between or on top of the concrete slabs and drinking water, beer and spirits. The clubbing Sunday is a blissful day.

It's about very particular communities which come together for the afternoon, the evening, and perhaps the following night too. They are largely formed through the feeling of drug solidarity. In the club and at night, drug consumption is always characterised by great secrecy. You have to smuggle the stuff in, then once you're in you have to go to the toilets to take it, and you don't want just anyone to be around.

Once it gets to the afternoon, things are different. The party after the actual party is no longer about the massive high, that's been and gone. Now it's essentially about not coming crashing down. Which means carefully topping up your dose to keep your level stable, coming down slowly, then perhaps stepping it up again in the evening, once your body clock has caught up again. Every high has a natural limit; it's an illusion to think you can keep it at its full intensity for a very long time. If you want to experience the highs, you have to get through the lows too. This is what the after-party is about: the fragile and shaky descent from the peaks you've previously reached, and the warm happy feeling of being exhausted yet fully alert. The night-time party is driven by its own energy; you have to provide the impetus for the next day.

Drugs play a part in this. Only a hard core of people are left over, a small raving community held together by a colourful weave of different feelings. There's that beautiful illusion of complete belonging which prompts you to share whatever you have left: drugs, money, cigarettes and drinks. If you go to the bar or to the petrol station, you bring something back for everyone. If you go to the cash machine, you take a little bit extra out. If someone's not made an appearance in a while, you go and check where they are and if they're doing OK.

This feeling of happiness and security amongst all your friends also has a dark underside: the fear that it might come to an end. The drugs might run out or someone might go home and allow the bubble of friendship, warmth and closeness in which you now feel so safe to burst. But these fears are relatively weak and can easily be kept in check. And besides, anyone who succumbs to the undercurrent of fear, or even begins thinking about what they have to do the next day, is almost on their way home already.

Even if you're no longer really high, the drugs still provide a gentle afterglow. The euphoria has faded, but you can still feel it. Far from being sober, you feel a pleasant weariness. The nucleus of energy which has powered you through the night is still glowing, but not as brightly. This is probably where the nice German raver expression of feeling **verstrahlt** (literally: 'exposed to radiation') comes from. It feels as if you've come too close to a very strong energy source and sustained minor damage through radioactive contamination.

In the nineties these after-party hours had their own soundtrack: ambient – a kind of **musica universalis** with no beats, intended for pleasant relaxation. Interestingly, this sound has almost completely died out today, and with it the chill-out rooms which used to be a feature of many clubs. Minimal techno and minimal house have taken its place – stripped down dance music based on simple and endless patterns of repetition.

It fits, because the after-party itself is life in a loop. The consumption which takes place on these afternoons does not tell a coming-of-age story. People don't 'experiment' with drugs here, as suggested by the jargon of repressive tolerance, which attempts to give meaning to drug-taking beyond the desire to get high. According to this logic, people take drugs in order to learn something about themselves. If you're carrying out an experiment, part of your personality has to remain sober – it has to take notes, learn something from the experience so that the high has not just been a waste of time. This is not what the after-party is about – it's about carrying on, aimless movement, squandering yourself, being pleasantly exhausted.

And ultimately these Sundays are also about going to Bar 25, the great adventure playground by the Spree. It's a little like visiting a battlefield when you approach the club on a fine Sunday afternoon. A few hundred metres away you see the first motionless figure sitting in the sun, then another, and then you go past two people who are holding each other up as they walk. In fact, there really is a multi-ethnic battle going on here: people from all over Europe have come together to combat boredom and fatigue, normality, decorum, and the need to go home. This is where you carry on.

Bar 25 is open all week long, but it's only from Sunday afternoon onwards that it reaches that state which has made it famous throughout the world. Clubbers have always stayed out for a long time in Berlin, but this is the first place where the after-party was drawn so decisively into the centre of the action. Bar 25 gave the after-party something about as fitting as white suits at a stoner party: glamour.

In fact, on a Sunday evening, this site by the Spree does bear a resemblance to a catwalk. One very slim guy is wearing short-sleeved overalls with a small red and white checked pattern. They look like his grandmother sewed them from the curtains of a northern German farmhouse. Another has a feather in his hair. A few girls are wearing dresses; others are sporting underwear garments from various decades. Some guys are cultivating the sleazy moustachioed look from gay pornos of the seventies. And one man, obviously at the tail-end of a hard weekend, looks like he's walked straight off the set of **Lord of the Rings**: it's Gollum having a bad hair day. You feel like you've landed at a fancy-dress ball where the organisers have accidentally put several different themes on the invitations: the twenties, glamour, vaudeville, circus girl, innocence. And in amongst them are people with the latest items from the collections of Berlin fashion designers.

Many little groups who have spent the first part of their Sunday together in a park, in the garden of a club or somewhere along the Spree end up here. Bar 25 has its very own rhythm. In other clubs you eventually get the feeling that it's time to leave. Here you arrive and you stay, stay a bit longer, perhaps fall asleep, wake up again half an hour later to find you're still here, maybe pick up the thread of a previous conversation, and stay a while longer. Sometimes much longer.

There is a high level of intimacy at Bar 25; you quickly get into conversations with other people, and considering the desperate state everyone appears to be in at first glance, it's actually surprising who you come into contact with on these 'radioactive' Sunday afternoons and evenings: a German girl who's a budding screenwriter; an assistant director who would like to become a film producer, also German (she has nothing to do with the screenwriter); a British-Swedish estate agent – she lives in Latin America; a guy on unemployment benefit who's German, lives in Berlin, and does odd jobs when people ask him to; a Spanish girl studying fashion. Added to these were a journalist, a web designer, a doctor, a music producer, a photographer – almost all people from the modern service industry, and most of them freelancers. People who, in some cases, work very hard and very long hours. All of them have been out since Saturday night, and all of them are going to stay a bit longer.

Could it be that the after-party, which has restructured the clubbing weekend, is linked to this way of life? To a life where the weekend no longer represents the counterpart to the working week – the goal to aim for during those days of alienated grafting in an office or a factory – but simply provides a break in the generally self-determined pattern of accomplishing various tasks, ultimately belonging to the same mode of existence?

The music certainly suggests that this is the case. It's minimal techno, not particularly loud – a sound which tends towards uniformity anyway, and this is accentuated by the lack of volume. Minimal doesn't build to climaxes, it foregoes any dramatic tension. It's music which is simply there. You latch onto the beat for a while, get on the dance floor, then go away again. Lots of people also talk while they're dancing, although this dancing would be better described as bopping along. Minimal is the direct extension of the music you play through your computer speakers whilst doing office work. A constant pulse, music for WLAN airports.

There is an alternative. In the 'Zirkus', a circus ring near the entrance, a DJ is playing the most bizarre assortment you could possibly imagine in this situation, a pot-pourri of dixieland, the greatest hits of the eighties – like 'Abracadabra' by The Steve Miller Band – and neofolk. At some point the dance floor is actually full, and the crowd are dancing to an old Tom Waits song with moves which would make you think it's techno. Everyone stays a bit longer.

72-hour party people: Bar 25

Partying like there's no tomorrow: the unlikely story of a party commune which runs the most famous after-party location in the world. Along with a hostel. And a restaurant. And a radio station. And a spa. In Bar 25, the lights never go out.

Bar 25 has a tough reputation, and it's well deserved. Sentences like 'I'm going back to the Bar to check if everything's OK,' or 'Then we went back to the Bar, and after that I'm not really sure,' or 'Somehow I lost my bag/my camera/my wallet/my keys/my mind there,' are classics of Berlin clubbing conversation. They all mean more or less the same thing: things got extremely messy. From the outside it creates an entirely different impression; the entrance looks more like something that would lead to a Western saloon with an allotment garden attached to it. The inconspicuous door in the pale fencing on Holzmarktstraße, in among the road traffic behind an S-Bahn bridge, also bears some resemblance to a gateway to hell. It's a repeating cycle. All summer long, Bar 25 is open non-stop from Friday evening to Monday afternoon, sometimes even to Tuesday morning. By Sunday afternoon, at the latest, things have always started getting out of hand. That's when the hardened party crowd start trickling in. And from Monday morning onwards at Bar 25, the art of excess is taken to probably unparalleled heights. This place has brought entirely new words into existence and provided the characters they describe with a space to express themselves. Evers since ravers have been around, there have been **Druffis** (people who are high on something). The same goes for **Verpeilte** (those who have literally 'lost their bearings'). But **Durchis** (those who are 'through' in the sense of 'finished'), is a Bar 25 coinage. You can imagine **Durchis** as **Druffis** who haven't been home in the time it's taken for their drugs to run out and the direct effects to have worn off.

There are all these stories from Bar 25, like the ones about girls who, on a Tuesday, can still remember that they gave someone a blowjob, but they're no longer sure who. Or about guys who walked into a tree while on the phone and are happy the next day when someone explains how they've ended up with such a bruise. Many have visited the confessional box built into the wall near the entrance, and would rather not be reminded what they got up to inside.

In fact, Bar 25 is a good deal more than this world-famous Mecca of messiness. It's a commune, a restaurant, a spa, a trailer park, a hostel, a cinema, a theatre and a catwalk. It's a projection screen, a political issue, a dream world and a work of art in the public sphere. Of course, the parties are the focus. But without the other activities, they wouldn't be possible. 'I always wanted to have everything, to experience everything. I always wanted to be everything. It wasn't enough for me to be a hippie, grow long dreads and go to Goa festivals, or to just hang around at art openings. I always wanted to do everything, and that's what I did. And that's what all the people here are like. We want to try to experience everything, to do everything,' says Christoph Klenzendorf, the charismatic founder, brains and front man of the Bar, when asked how the various spheres fit together. 'I'm an aesthete. I have a need to make things beautiful. For friends, for guests, for people who come to visit me. For us, this is a basic requirement.'

Bar 25 is a radical project – you could call it radical pop. It's self-determined, experimental, geared towards direct, immediately palpable effect, and it's successful, very successful even – a lived utopia. The Bar has made waves throughout the world; people are talking about this place in Zurich, Tokyo, Miami, Buenos Aires and New York. One reason is that it has nurtured its own musical style, a minimal sound which perfectly suits the open-air bar situation, where the volume is never allowed to exceed a certain level due to the neighbours across the river and the people sleeping in the trailers – a sound which has been successfully exported around the world and which, when heard in a different kind of setting, often sounds as out of place as gangsta rap at a high school prom.

But it's not the music which has made Bar 25 so famous. It's the way that the founders have made no compromises in their mission of constructing their very own world on this picturesque spot on the banks of the Spree, in the middle of the German capital. It's a world where excessive partying through to Monday night is not at odds with running a restaurant which attracts a different crowd of its own: lawyers, tax advisors, Mitte snobs, fashion junkies, MTV presenters, B-list celebs. Finally, the spa has its very own crowd too: spiritualists who like to be massaged to New Age music and think it's a great pleasure to be able to step out of the sauna and into a natural setting, here in the middle of the city.

'That's really funny,' says Klenzendorf. 'On Monday evening you have the most twisted individuals here, the sickest party you can imagine. Then you go to sleep, and on Tuesday people come to the restaurant and spend two hundred euros on a meal. You think to yourself, if they only knew what was going on here 24 hours ago! But I think it's great that we have a place for everyone.' Then there are the regular open-air cinema screenings. 'Look at the cinephiles who are into this. They watch films, then they have endless discussions about how interesting they find some technique or other. There's space for them, too.'

Where we come from, what we want

The story of Bar 25 begins in the nineties. For the scene which inhabited the numerous legal and illegal bars all over Mitte back then, partying was always a full-time job rather that a weekend activity. One of these bars, which were named after days of the week, was always bound to be open; there was always a party going on in some basement or on a deserted piece of land, and in the summer there were festivals large and small out in the country. Christoph Klenzendorf, who's actually a photographer, was one of these people you used to bump into all over the place. Rave was a principle of life – in the shared flat where Klenzendorf lived, the doors were always open and everyone was welcome. 'That's at the heart of everything: partying,' he says. This hasn't changed. At some point he got tired of just going to other people's parties, he says. He wanted to do something of his own. He and a partner got hold of an old campervan and converted it into a mobile bar.

They went round to illegal parties and sold drinks, including trips to 'Fusion', a huge outdoor rave in Brandenburg.

They did this for two years before deciding to look for something permanent. That's when they got lucky. The Berlin sanitation department (BSR) was looking for a temporary tenant for a plot of land by the Spree near the Michaelkirchbrücke bridge. It's a huge site – 10,000 square metres – and the costs were too high to cover through open-air events. At the time when Klenzendorf made his enquiry, the BSR had just lost several potential investors. He suggested renting just part of the site, and the BSR was happy to have finally found a tenant.

And so, in August 2004, the story of Bar 25 began with a marathon six-week party, at the end of which they concluded: yes, that was great, but we need more structure. 'There weren't any rules back then; the place was only semi-legal; nothing had been approved by the building authorities except for one trailer we were using as a bar. We partied non-stop for six weeks; no one knew what was going on. After that we could see – yes that was fun, but just techno, just partying, it's not enough.' Besides, they had become friends with Juval Dieziger, a chef who had previously worked at the restaurant of the Mitte club Cookies. They decided to join forces. 'I've always travelled a lot, just like the others here,' explains Klenzendorf. 'In the winter, while walking in Nepal, I was sat in a hut and I thought to myself, I want something like this. So we got together in February and said, let's make a restaurant, and a hostel as well. One thing led to another, and in 2005 we got started.'

That basically covers the most important ingredients: acting with confidence on a gut feeling that what's right for you will work for everyone else too; ignoring all naysayers who sneer, 'It'll never work, what are you gonna serve up, currywurst?' And above all, an attitude which favours going ahead and doing things over having a master plan. This is how the Bar was created, and this is how it has grown. The Zirkus was added when Germany hosted the football world cup. It was intended as an arena for watching the matches, but the stage meant that it was also suitable for concerts and cinema screenings. When a request for a sauna cropped up, they created the spa area. The latest development is a self-built oven for making stone-baked pizza. Bar 25 is a parallel world not only for its guests, but also for its residents. When they leave the site, they say, 'I'm going into town.'

In fact, if you've only been to Bar 25 at the weekend, you'll only have got to know part of the site: the party adventure playground between the door and the bar, the after-hour stomping ground by the Spree with the small circus arena on the left, the pizza station by the water, the wooden benches with a river view, the famous swing hanging from its tree and the dance floor in the log cabin.

The site of Bar 25 is considerably larger, however, than the area frequented by the party crowd at the weekend. Behind the bar in the cabin is a door leading to a drinks store, and behind this is a car park. Around the car park are the trailers where some of the crew live. You can pick up a trailer like this for a couple of hundred euros; you just have to look in the classified ads magazine **Zweite Hand**. There's a shared shower block and a toilet trailer. If you continue a little further you suddenly find yourself in a small wooded area: trees and undergrowth all around, with a trail leading through the middle. There are a few modest houses too. Christoph Klenzendorf lives in one with his girlfriend; others are rented out.

This is the famous hostel. Quentin Tarantino is amongst its previous guests. Klenzendorf's little house was once the hut of a brothel keeper in Brandenburg. He bought it on eBay for one euro. There's something idyllic about the place: brushing your teeth here in the morning by the Spree in you bare feet – it's a nice thought. After all, you're still in the middle of the city.

In his 1985 book of the same name, Hakim Bey coined the term 'temporary autonomous zone', which perfectly describes the many illegal raves and mobile clubs which characterised Berlin's night life in the nineties. It also fits Bar 25. It's temporary, and somehow everyone accepts that the magic won't last forever, and it's certainly autonomous.

On the other hand, the summer of 2008 marked its fifth year, and the restaurant business is professionally run. When we order something from one of the bars on this Thursday afternoon, the barwoman asks Christoph Klenzendorf for money. She's speaking English. He looks at her somewhat puzzled and says, 'I don't pay. I'm Christoph. I'm running this place.' – 'Oh,' she says, 'okay'. 'That's a disappointment,' I say. 'I thought you were one big commune where everyone knows each other.' – 'Me too,' he says, 'it's just that it's got quite big.' We take our drinks and sit by the water. In fact, he explains, although they want the kind of independence which would allow them all to provide for themselves, it just doesn't add up in business terms. 'Lots of people think we wheel barrow-loads of cash out of here. That's rubbish. When I look at the turnover, I think to myself, where does all the money go? The difference between here and any other club is that elsewhere you can close the door and your costs stop there. Except for the rent, of course. Here you have twenty to forty people permanently on the site who are living from that money.' And drinking the bar dry with their mates.

We don't call it work

The history of subcultures is full of such attempts to fuse life and work into a new, alternative, non-alienated form of existence. One of these is portrayed by the Berlin author Bernd Cailloux in his novel **Das Geschäftsjahr 68/69** (The 68/69 Business Year). The group calls itself a **Mußegesellschaft**, or leisure society, and Cailloux depicts the business-hippies' moments of happiness as well as the insurmountable obstacles they come up against in trying to merge their office hours with their leisure time. In a certain respect, the novel also tells a prehistory of techno: the leisure society founds its business upon the invention of the strobe light, and the story takes place in Düsseldorf, in a scene from which Kraftwerk was to emerge a few years later. The enterprise fails because those involved can't agree whether they're in it to work or to live.

Having talked to Christoph Klenzendorf, you get the feeling that there really is such a thing as subcultural progress – the contradiction between work and life has been removed in Bar 25, and without leisure time simply being consumed in work. Klenzendorf and his friends demonstrate that self-exploitation isn't necessarily the price you have to pay for self-determination. 'We're part of society; we have to earn money; we have to earn our daily bread,' he says. 'But we want to do it in a way which gives us satisfaction. And I'm rather proud that with the things I enjoy, which are basically leisure activities – having fun, partying – that I've managed to make a living and earn some money out of it. We call it 'hippie de luxe'. It's a hippie lifestyle with trailers, in the open air, with shared showers – a commune – but we also live like kings: the best food, all the drinks we need, a sauna, a space for partying. We have everything. We are actually hippies, in the touchy-feely sense, but we nevertheless enjoy the finer things in life.'

I am a circus child

Are there any negative aspects? A couple. For one thing, you have to be strong if you want to live at Bar 25. 'People push themselves to their limits here,' says Klenzendorf. 'Some people can't cope with it any more after a while. That's when they go under. Plus you have some people who feel like they're part of it when in fact they're not. It can be a quick process, people drifting away. Then sometimes you have to say to others, "Listen, I'm not going to look after you when it's over at this place." There have also been some people who we've had to ask to leave.' These are questions and problems that every shared flat or commune has to battle with at some point. It's just that here the energy level is higher.

Another thing is that not everyone enjoys watching grown adults turn into children again. This happens several times every weekend; it goes with the territory. Bar 25 is an adventure playground. It has a swing, a coin-operated bucking bronco, a bumper car you can sit in. It also bears some resemblance to a circus and all that goes with it – people, animals, sensations. The attraction of this club surely has a lot to do with the age-old story of the circus child which is so deeply rooted in Western consciousness, the story of the kid from a good family who escapes the constraints of convention by running away from home to join the circus and to live a life of freedom with this new, chosen family.

Bar 25 is a place that people long for in a similar way. Those that run away from home can find the freedom here to lead another life. It's a fact that many of those who end up here at the weekend are middle-class kids. Fallen middle-class kids, perhaps, and from all parts of the world. As diverse as it looks, the social makeup is actually very narrow, at least from an outside perspective. Perhaps this place is simply too queer for working-class kids, or perhaps their idea of a raver's paradise is less marked by images of innocence.

This is not a criticism of what goes on at Bar 25, but perhaps a criticism of the self-image of many of its guests – the club isn't actually as diverse and open as it feels. The people here just look that way.

But as far as this look goes, they don't do things by halves. Their style has added entirely new ingredients to Berlin night life. No one went clubbing in fancy dress in post-reunification Berlin. Unless they were going to the Love Parade. Or for sexual reasons. But the fetish scene generally had its own clubs. There was very little overlapping in the nineties, and hardly any at all in the noughties. Berlin was in the protestant heartland, not carnival territory. 'Fancy dress? You what?'

At Bar 25, things are very different. Perhaps it comes down to the way Berlin's fashion sense has evolved. In any case, the line between fashion and fancy dress is blurred, particularly among those who don't have a lot of money and therefore shop at second-hand stores and flea markets. Indeed, with their knee-high stockings, flat caps and old shoes, many of the guys at Bar 25 look like they purchased their outfits from a jumble sale at an old-people's home. The girls paint a similar picture, although their style of dress often features a touch of the burlesque. In keeping with the circus motif of the whole place, many girls at Bar 25 look like they've just come from a party themed on 'vaudeville', or 'heaven', or 'baroque'.

The most essential thing, however, is glitter make-up. At some point the first girls started turning up to Bar 25 with glitter on their faces. Sometimes just a smidge, but sometimes applied more copiously and prominently, to highlight the cheekbones for instance. Then a few of the guys started doing it too. Girls began combining the glitter with little angel wings which they wore on their back. A backlash followed, with people turning up in 'Glitter My Ass' T-shirts they'd had printed. Not that this lessened the allure of glitter fever. In 2008, glitter-smeared faces could be seen in all Berlin's clubs. In 2009 it may have spread right across Europe.

The glitter make-up symbolises the great ambivalence of the way of life that Bar 25 stands for – the underlying fantasy of innocence, the desire to regress, the escapism: Oh, how I'd love to be a prima ballerina, a princess, a fairy. And at the same time, there's an assertion of one's own outsider status: Yes, I'm different, but if just a few of us get together we'll be fine.

And when it comes down to it, Bar 25 is also about an unexpected friendship between two local scenes. In the nineties there was always a clear division between the Goa scene, favoured by those who felt most comfortable at an open-air rave somewhere in Brandenburg, and the city ravers, who wanted to party in clubs. This wasn't just a question of the music: the Goa sound, with its clear roots in trance, was fairly incompatible with the styles which accompanied most parties in the city's clubs. The two groups were also clearly distinguished through their lifestyle choices: the former were hippies, the latter weren't. Bar 25 merged these two scenes to form something new. This little club by the Spree, with its natural and urban environment, is both an indoor and an outdoor rave. Underneath the disco ball which hangs from the large tree in front of the main cabin, you feel like you've just landed in an Olafur Eliasson art installation. And the whole thing only works because there's an inside and an outside, because the borders aren't open to everyone. The radical inclusivity of Bar 25 begins and ends at the door. During the week it's not difficult to get in, partly thanks to the numerous concerts and cinema screenings, the restaurant and the spa. At the weekend, however, the door goes from wide open to closed, and the doorwoman takes up her position.

The people running the Bar know that their door is feared, and in principle they don't like it either. At first anyone could come in here, but as time went by entry was made increasingly difficult. For understandable reasons: if you're offering your guests a space of extreme liberty, you have to build a high protective wall.

'Sunday is the day for friends. For the people where you say, "Yes, you fit." The atmosphere here on Sundays, I've never experienced it anywhere else. The way you come along and everyone does their own thing, plays their own games, but keeps it cool. No one pushes it beyond the limits, so it's not too much for other people to handle. That's something to behold. That's the kind of thing I'm into. You know, everyone's a freak.'

All are equal behind the decks

Interestingly, the music at Bar 25 plays a different role to the music in all other Berlin clubs. The sound is a constant pulse, simply there, part of the atmosphere. This is partly down to the fact that they can't turn it up very loud, but it's not just that. The parties here have no beginning and no end, they just carry on and on. Besides, if you've already been pounded by several days of clubbing beats, you don't want anything too loud or intense. But you are happy to hear mini splashes of melody, playful sounds which you can follow and look forward to as they appear and disappear like little acoustic glow-worms. Those who are after something more direct will sooner or later end up in the Zirkus, where bands sometimes play (unless they're lying in the corner wasted) or where DJs play quite different music.

'We pay laughable performance fees,' says Klenzendorf, 'but at least everyone gets the same. 200 euros for everyone. It makes no difference if it's a star like Richie Hawtin or some unknown DJ. We don't make any distinction.' Interestingly, this very policy makes Bar 25 (just like Club der Visionäre, which is of a similar nature in many respects) so incredibly attractive for well-known DJs: to not be the star for once, to be treated perfectly normally. Where else would Richie Hawtin get an earful from two girls at the bar who have no idea who he is? They told him he'd better watch his manners and not push in the queue.

You have to imagine this from the perspective of the extremely famous DJs: they're not only artists, they're also akin to professional athletes or gladiators. They have two options. Either they get to a point where they decide to go completely straight, maybe have a couple of beers, but otherwise steer clear of all drugs. Or they don't. In this case, they're constantly exposed to temptation, and the drugs and alcohol which club promoters around the world lay on for star DJs aren't from the same batch as the gear your average raver gets his mitts on. Someone who's been DJing for years might not be able to do it any other way. It's impossible to summon the same enthusiasm for the music three times a weekend over a period of years – unless you have some good drugs. This doesn't have to be viewed as cynicism. It's more of a practical necessity, and it can become extremely strenuous, too.

This is why many of the DJs who are very successful in the business and earn a lot of money go to a health resort once or twice a year. Depending on their mentality and how badly intoxicated they feel, they might go for stirred water therapy at a New-Age spa resort, or opt for the brutal efficiency of a kidney dialysis holiday. Being able to get thoroughly mashed and nevertheless look fresh is simply part of the job profile. And of course, every local promoter wants to get off their rocker with a star, just like every small-town librarian wants to take the famous author to the local Italian when they come for a reading. This is one of the reasons why people become club promoters in the first place. And this is why the DJs like coming to Bar 25 so much: there aren't any of those people around. They can party there without being stars.

Bar 25's egalitarian attitude is also aided by the fact that its non-stop parties create a huge demand for DJs. As such, everyone gets the same fee – plus a generous helping of extra goodies: once, the story goes, little survival kits for every DJ were hung from a washing line, filled with condoms, drinks tokens and all sorts of essentials for days of happy partying.

Half a ton of confetti

The parties that the Bar organises for its own celebrations are legendary. Not only because of the varied and extravagant decorations, but also because of the lavish buffets and all-round catering. Even DJs who've seen their fair share of excess in their professional lives go wide-eyed when recalling these parties where everything is in abundance, but where the most important thing is not the brand of champagne, as so often when a club throws a big bash and the main object of the event is to show the world what luxuries they can afford. The special thing here is the way that all these things are shared naturally and with such pleasure. Hippie de luxe, like the man says. They're close to nature, they celebrate life as a community, but they don't have an ethic or aesthetic of abstinence.

The best example of this is the half ton of confetti which was launched into the air at a Bar 25 birthday party. Coupled with a light installation, it created mesmerising optical effects. After a certain time in the Zirkus you were standing almost knee-deep in confetti and it seemed like the most normal thing in the world. The route over to Ostbahnhof was strewn with bits of paper for days afterwards. This kind of stunt is not a necessity. Another promoter would probably have held on to the 2,000 euros that it cost. Not Bar 25.

'We started with nothing,' says Christoph Klenzendorf, summing up the history of Bar 25. 'We didn't have a penny. In the first year, we borrowed 5,000 euros from a friend which we spent on screws and machinery. We nicked all the wood from various building sites. We started from nothing, and now we're here. We can afford to have everything we want now. To a point, of course – we're not millionaires. But we can afford leisure. To excel in the art of living is to forego the important things in life so you can afford what is superfluous. This also applies to what we're doing here. We go without the most important things: there are people here who have no health insurance, but they drink the finest champagnes. The post-war society, our parents, would say, "You're crazy. Make sure that your teeth are okay and that you have bread on the table." And what we want is champagne, only the best, and then we'll see what comes our way.'

News from where the grass is greener

Resident Advisor and the changing structure of the pop culture public

DJs are sought-after people. Just look at a well-known DJ when he enters a club. He rarely arrives alone; most of the time he has a whole entourage with him. Friends, acquaintances, girlfriends, managers – all these people come attached to the DJ. Maybe they want to bathe in his limelight, see themselves reflected in his sex appeal, or perhaps it's just a matter of getting in for free. The circus continues when the famous DJ starts his set. People scramble for space around the DJ booth, shout things in his ear, smile, wiggle their hips. They fetch him drinks, sort out drugs, light his cigarettes. The area around the DJ booth can be a hotly contested space. Guys come up and ask, 'What was that last tune again?' Girls want to be in the centre of the action, and that's where the DJ is. Everyone else is oriented around him.

Things can function differently, however. If you observe Paul Clement in a club, for instance, you see an entirely different situation. Clement is a co-founder and one of the managers of Resident Advisor. DJs are drawn to him like bees to honey. 'Alright, Paul? How's it going? Have you heard so-and-so's new record? What else did you get up to last weekend?'

Resident Advisor is the leading online magazine for the techno and house scene. It's not that Resident Advisor can make or break DJ careers. In the case of house and techno, this power still lies squarely with clubbers themselves. However, the site may well have more influence on these musical career paths than other media.

RA, as Resident Advisor calls itself, is another element of the scene which has followed the buzz to Berlin. It opened a branch office here in summer 2009. It's located on one floor of an old building in Mitte, an area where squatters and artists settled in the nineties and which is now home to galleries and agencies. It's spacious, with high ceilings, white walls and a few desks. On the wall are two large banners with the RA logo, and in the corner is a pair of decks.

At first glance you're amazed at how tidy the place is. Then you realise why the desks look so orderly: there isn't a single sheet of paper in the whole office. Welcome to the digital present.

RA is a kind of portal for the European house and techno scene, and it's a flourishing company. It was founded in Australia in 2001, but the managers soon moved over to England, and now they're running operations from London, Berlin and Sydney. Covering roughly 200 regions around the world, the site offers addresses and listings of clubs and other events which are broadly related to the techno scene – and in recent times these listings have become almost encyclopaedic in detail. Since going online, RA has announced around 120,000 events, says Clement, and half of these were in the year 2008 alone. That's 60,000 opportunities to go out and dance, and the listings cover all corners of the world, although there is a particular focus on London, Berlin, Amsterdam, New York, Sydney and California. These are the places with the highest concentrations of RA users and RA-listed events.

At first glance, Resident Advisor is a well-produced digital blend of two old analogue media: the city listings guide and the music magazine. Its thematic spectrum has been reduced to electronic music only, but the geographical scope has been expanded so as to encompass the entire world rather than a single city. Looking at the situation more closely, however, RA is part of a new approach to locality.

We are seeing a change in how the pop culture public is structured, and this is being driven by two related processes. Firstly, there's the internet, the digitisation of information and all that goes with it. Secondly, there's the liberation of pop cultures from national frameworks. For some time now, pop cultures have been organised through networks which are both global and local, hence the term 'glocal' coined by cultural commentators. Electronic music provides a wonderful example of how a glocal public can function.

The local side of this public has many different faces: the great techno conversation emanates from the clubs themselves – you have to be there to participate. But from here it spreads to record stores, cafés and bars, newspaper reports and smaller Berlin websites.

It's through a site like Resident Advisor that this local public is fed into the global sphere. You can safely assume that some young internet surfers in, let's say, Toronto, without ever having been to Berlin, are better informed about the line-up at a certain techno club on a certain night than, for example, the builder who listens to heavy metal but lives a few minutes away from Berghain.

Resident Advisor is also part of another development which has turned music journalism on its head in recent years. For the internet is not only faster than printed media, it also offers unlimited space. The articles and interviews featured on RA are often longer than their equivalents in music magazines.

There's a history behind this development. First came the blog, the home-made internet platform which, around the turn of the century, reached great popularity amongst young music writers who didn't want their enthusiasm to be stifled by the conventions of the printed press. Here they could write about music without editorial restrictions or controls. Then at some point many of these bloggers began uploading the music files they were writing about to their websites. The mp3 blog was born. Nowadays only a small number of bloggers still do this, presumably due to complaints from the labels. Since these are fans writing about music, an email from one of their favourite small labels probably had a more lasting effect than any threats of being chased up by the lawyers of the major labels. Instead, the music is now streamed. This means that visitors to the blog can still listen to it, but it's not so easy to download.

Then there are podcasts. A great number of sites have started offering these now, more or less legally. Resident Advisor is one of them. It takes older podcasts offline after four weeks and pays royalties in the same way as an internet radio station. Dozens of web sites do a similar thing. Some are clubs which present the upcoming DJ bookings with mixes (like Bunker in New York). Some are music enthusiasts who conduct detailed interviews with DJs and ask them to make mixes to put on the site (like littlewhiteearbuds.com) Some are collectives of music aficionados who put mixes on their site to promote the music they love (like infinitestatemachine.com) or music journalists who complement their blog with mixes from highly rated DJs (like houseisafeeling.com).

Thanks to these new structures, a new kind of public is forming, one which is organised without regard for national boundaries. As when the low-cost airlines opened up a new space which made the distinction between domestic and international travel redundant, and as when the single European currency brought the member states a step closer together, here we can see a discursive space which is completely open to all Europeans – provided they speak English, of course.

For British pop culture, this may not appear to be a particularly novel development. British magazines have found a readership all over Europe since the sixties – many young German, French or Danish people may have learned English reading **Melody Maker** or discovered fashions presented in **i-D** or **The Face**. For continental Europeans, however, the ease with which we can gain insight into other local scenes is something new.

Nevertheless, the fact that old hierarchies have been broken down doesn't mean there aren't any power structures in place. The cards have been reshuffled, and Berlin has emerged as a capital of cool.

Subcultures are often cultures of longing: how we would love to be in another place, maybe even in another time, to be of a different skin colour or a different sex. These are cultures for domestic consumption. You can study them, listen to the records, watch films or read books about them, but you can never be part of them.

Much of the European fascination for Afro-American pop cultures works in this way, and so does the Germans' love of British pop. It's a commonly shared feeling among German music fans that we'll never have such good bands as the British. The melancholy resignation that the grass must be greener on the other side has always been at the centre of German teenagers' attraction to those bands who grace the pages of the British music press on a weekly basis. And anyone who's talked to a British krautrock fan knows that the very same process can work in reverse. These are dream cultures.

Electronic music is also full of these distant desires. The fanfares which accompany the arrival in Europe of any record by a producer from Detroit can largely be attributed to a belief in the existence of this magical place from which we Europeans are unfortunately excluded and which we can only access by buying the music.

Many of the music blogs about techno and house follow a similar pattern, and sometimes the great techno worlds imagined by bloggers produce new realities of their own. After all, music technology is cheap and producing your own tracks is not so hard, and so the semi-serious musical genre 'blog house' has emerged. This describes a situation where music is made by people sitting in front of their computers for other people sitting in front of their computers. You might call it conversational music; there's no one dancing here. Or daydream music – for people who'd like to be somewhere else.

Interestingly, Berlin night life and everything related to it is a dream culture and a place that people all over the world long to be. For Germans, this is quite a new situation, and it's a factor which is drawing many outsiders to the city.

You could take this line of thought a little further. The futurism which fuelled the endeavours of many techno producers, activists and DJs in the nineties has vanished into thin air since the turn of the century. If this attitude still exists at all, then it's in reference to the past. However, the techno scene as a whole is still looking firmly forwards.

In an interview with **Spex** magazine in summer 2007, the pop theorist Diedrich Diederichsen said, 'The culture industry of the future will work with outdoor formats. These will be formats where being outside will involve an incredibly flexible interaction with precisely defined music, clothing, visuals and so on. These phenomena of which we still have limited experience – mobile parties, flash mobs and so on – will be industrialised. People will arrange to meet up somewhere or follow each other 'gotcha' style, and this activity will be accompanied by a soundtrack and a narrative framework, though one which is not too sharply defined – which will allow all those participating to play an active, intervening role.'

This is a fairly accurate description of what happens every weekend in the area between Friedrichshain and Kreuzberg. People arrange to meet up and listen to music, indulge in nonsense, move through this landscape of adventure, share intense experiences, and sometimes test their own limits along the way. Above all, those present have an 'active, intervening role' to play in almost everything that happens. Resident Advisor (and of course other sites) can be thought of as an interface, a linking and orientation tool which helps you to join up the dots of your weekend.

Berlin abroad

Berlin clubbing culture touring the hotspots of its global proliferation: on the road in Barcelona with the Berlin DJ and musician Efdemin.

It's not only nights out clubbing that have been transformed by the Easyjet revolution in recent years. The crowd are not the only ones to have gained greater mobility since the nineties. Back then you really had to be a big name to get booked at foreign clubs every weekend. In the noughties, regular international bookings arrived in the mid-market of the clubbing business. Consequently, you're all the more likely to bump into DJs at airports; they're the guys and girls with the record bags over their shoulders and the dark bags under their eyes. If you think their lives are all one big party in glamorous club land, you're wrong. They're mostly spent in hotel rooms and airports, waiting for connections and hanging around.

And so it is for Phillip Sollmann one afternoon in June 2008 at Barcelona airport. It's the Monday after the Sonar festival where Sollmann played two gigs. We're waiting for the flight back to Berlin and we meet all the other DJs who are also waiting for their flights. There's the DJ from Rome with his girlfriend and a promoter who runs a small club; a club promoter from Austria; another from Frankfurt with his two friends; two fellow DJs from Berlin, one girl one guy; a group of DJs, label managers and artists from Cologne. Everyone swaps updates on how things are going at the various clubs. Most of them know each other because they've played together somewhere once. This club has just had some trouble from the police, that one's about to close, another no one's heard about for quite a while. Or there are the other conversations: 'We have to play together again some time.' – 'Ah, back to Berlin. Are you going to Bar 25 later?' – 'Where did you play?' – 'Where did Hendrik get to anyway?'

Hendrik is Hendrik Weber; he played a live set at Sonar as Pantha du Prince. He and Sollmann help to run Dial Records, a label founded in Hamburg in the late nineties. Weber lives in Paris, Sollmann in Berlin. Dial co-founder Peter Kersten, alias Lawrence, has stayed in Hamburg where he also runs a record shop and organises club nights. The fourth member of the alliance is David Lieske, alias Carsten Jost, who moved to Tel Aviv in November 2008. Pop has always been an international venture, but the way that it's now so natural for a small artist label to be run as a network spanning four countries may be something new.

Sonar probably couldn't have earned itself the reputation it has now without the low-cost airlines either. It began in the mid-nineties as a small beach event; now it's the most famous electronic music festival in Europe. Of course, this is also down to its highly ambitious and illustrious line-ups, and to Barcelona itself, a city with a quite unique blend of upper-class charm and small-time criminality. Nevertheless, the whole event would not come together on this scale if it weren't so cheap to get there – and that goes for both the visitors and the artists. Based on the promise that an appearance at Sonar will raise their profile and thus increase their market value, the event organisers don't pay most artists a performance fee.

Sonar has such a good reputation because it has succeeded, year upon year, in combining a weekend of hedonism with a challenging programme of music. The inner-city festival site plays host to more subtle sound experiments in the afternoons and early evenings. At night the event gets turned up a few notches. The large-scale night-time rave serves to cross-finance the squealing guitar experiments and laptop bleeps and bloops on the daytime programme. It's an event which still holds the charm of a high-tech folk festival while it's dark, but makes a considerably more apocalyptic impression once the sun comes up. Screaming people are waving in the direction of the stage; topless Englishmen with lobster-red skin lie sleeping in corners; the floor is littered with empty plastic cups and bottles. In the neighbouring arenas the first commando clean-up team is starting to sweep up the debris just as Phillip Sollmann cranks up the volume once more.

It's half past five in the morning and he's the last act of the night to grace this stage which has been set up between two giant exhibition halls on a site near the airport. There are around three thousand people still here. They cheer as Sollmann puts on his first record.

It's a pleasure to watch him at work. He hangs onto the mixer with his long arms and lurches back and forth as if the frequencies were tossing him around in a rough sea. It's as if his body were hooked up to the system just like the speakers. At one point one of the monitor speakers comes loose from its fixing and crashes to the floor half a metre from his left foot. The record skips; Sollmann looks up in surprise, then at the record – it's still playing, no drama. Then he looks out at the crowd and pumps his fist to get them going. The dance floor cheers, and he turns around to rummage through his bags for the next record. It's brutal, uplifting, a full-on rave with all the trimmings. No one leaves, and although the stage manager signals several times for him to wrap things up, the records keep on coming.

This kind of large-scale rave relies on some remarkable logistics. For instance, if you have five large stages, each with an eight-hour programme of music, then you need a great deal of space to accommodate all the artists. A whole wing of the exhibition halls has been partitioned off into enclosures. There are around ten of these on the corridor where Phillip Sollmann and Hendrik Weber are based. The names of the DJs are displayed on notes pinned to the door of each room. These are the big names in techno, from Ricardo Villalobos to Miss Kittin. All of them have brought their own entourage of people who hang around in the corridor and work their way through the cool boxes of beer, vodka and energy drinks which are provided in the artists' enclosures. Since the festival site is fairly large, a driver takes you in a minibus from the backstage area to behind the actual stage. It's quite an experience if you're not accustomed to it.

Phillip Sollmann and Hendrik Weber are new to this league. Their Sonar performance is the high point of their extraordinary careers to date. 'It really is completely crazy,' Sollmann says later. 'Two years ago I was still organising parties in the basement of Festsaal Kreuzberg where only five people turned up if things went badly, stuff like that.' Weber also shakes his head in disbelief as we're standing at the back of the stage during Efdemin's set: 'It feels like we just smuggled our way in here.'

When you're playing an early-morning set, once the crowd has already been thoroughly warmed up by the other DJs, it's quite difficult to maintain a balance between your self-respect and the urge to simply rave to the max – especially in front of such a huge mass of people. You're left with no choice but to keep on triggering the simplest of reflexes. Subtler forms of communication between the DJ and the dance floor are no longer feasible at this point. Not with wrecked heads like this guy with the hat, the eyes like saucers and the backstage pass who keeps making hand signals which no one else can understand, first from the dance floor and then from the edge of the stage. Bass out, bass back in, hands in the air, everyone cheers, everything's hunky-dory. This basic principle of pounding out a big set while still letting your signature sound shine through is a fine art. 'And I didn't play any rubbish records!' exclaims a laughing Phillip Sollmann as he walks back from the front of the stage at the end of his set, having received the adulation of the crowd.

The minibus drops us off at the entrance to the backstage area. Sollmann still wants to meet a friend of his from London, but he's lost on the site somewhere and doesn't surface, despite the hectic phone calls and precise directions. Some other people do appear though, including a couple of rather sloshed English girls with large sunglasses from the entourage of another DJ. Somehow the group has to be divided between the few minibuses that are available. These things can take a while at eight on a Sunday morning under the already baking Barcelona sun – especially when no one has stayed sober. Eventually we get our lift back to the hotel in the city centre, where the streets have begun to give off quite a glare under the blue morning sky. It's half past eight; I go to bed.

Sollmann tells me later that he went back out again, to an afterparty in a warehouse somewhere in the north of the city. Conveniently, he arrived at the same moment as Ricardo Villalobos, who was booked to play there. Apparently dozens of people were standing around Villalobos shouting 'Ricardo, Ricardo'. This clearly annoyed him, so he made his way towards the back entrance with everyone following. At the door he then pointed to five people – you, you, you, you and you – and went in with the chosen few, one of which was Sollmann. And so he entered this rave hell, a fairly large place with several rooms where the temperature was around fifty degrees, a few hundred people were dancing, the girls were wearing bikinis and had streams of sweat trickling between their breasts, the guys' shirts were soaked and stuck to their chests, the toilet had overflowed, and on the floor the toilet water was mixing with the sweat and the condensation dripping from the ceiling. A few people were lying in puddles and grinning. There was a hole in one of the windows which a man was hanging out of so he could suck in some fresh air. It was all a bit much. He left after a few minutes.

Phillip Sollmann's career has run an unusual course. He comes from Kassel, in central Germany, and moved to Hamburg in the mid-nineties, lured like so many others at that time by the famous combination of pop-music discourse and hard drinking. Sollmann also played in a band and sang in German, which was the done thing in Hamburg at the time. However, when he noticed one night during a gig at Pudel Club that the Blumfeld singer and scene VIP Jochen Distelmeyer was in the crowd, he became aware of the limitations of what he and his band were doing. He began making electronic music, and soon one of the tracks he released with his production partner Alexander Polzin under the alias Tobin ended up on the first sampler compilation of the newly founded Cologne label Kompakt – now one of the largest and best-known German techno labels on the world stage.

That was in 1999. Techno as a mass phenomenon had collapsed;

the music was going back underground; a new generation of producers, DJs and label managers began forming their networks. Many of the labels which were to shape the sound of the noughties came into existence around this time. In 1999 it was by no means a foregone conclusion that the techno scene would become heavily focused on Berlin a few years later. Kompakt was founded in Cologne, Dial in Hamburg, and Perlon had already been around for a while in Frankfurt. As for Phillip Sollmann, he disappeared to Vienna for a while to study acoustical engineering at the performing arts university there.

European networks

Dial is a remarkable label. Not only because it has such an international structure and has released around fifty records without having a label office, a warehouse or even an address, but also because it has such a broad cultural basis. Having been born out of the Hamburg scene, Dial can effortlessly combine pop and left-wing politics into an attitude which also allows the people involved to be well dressed. Plus, as part of the Berlin constellation, Dial is open for connections with the visual arts. 'Dial grows wild,' says Sollmann. 'If someone wants to do something, they just do it.' Each of the managers agrees to take their turn at running the label for a while, he explains. In spring 2007, two albums were released within a few weeks of each other which gave Weber's and Sollmann's careers the crucial boost, propelling them towards that gig in Barcelona: **This Bliss** by Pantha du Prince, and **Efdemin**.

Phillip Sollmann's artistic universe differs considerably from that of most other techno producers and DJs. Not only did he study acoustical engineering, he also once created a sound installation in collaboration with a soprano singer in a Munich apartment belonging to the film director Rainer Werner Fassbinder. And in the tunnel entrance to the villa of the French silent film diva Musidora he constructed a complex drone, a sustained tone which you could only hear when you stood at a certain point in the room. In 2007 he taught as a guest lecturer at a French university and played long drones to the students in lectures.

When we meet in a small restaurant near the festival site the evening before his performance, I ask him about the gigs he recently played in the USA, particularly the set he played in Detroit, but he's more interested in talking about New York. He says he was finally able to visit the Dream House of the legendary minimalist music pioneer LaMonte Young. Phillip Sollmann loves his music, as well as that of the composer Alvin Lucier. A great deal has been written about the relationship between modern classical music and techno, most of which is nonsense. In the exceptional case of Efdemin, however, minimalist music and minimal techno really do belong together. **Something Is Missing**, the only record Sollmann has released under his real name, is an album full of drones.

It's a pleasant, interesting meal, not least because it reveals a slice of Easyjet cosmopolitanism. Sollmann and Weber are there, as well as a young Israeli DJ who's a big fan of Dial and has just moved from Tel Aviv to Berlin, and his girlfriend who's German and lives in Berlin but grew up in Barcelona. We are also joined by a friend of Sollmann's from when he lived in Barcelona for three months to complete an art project several years ago, and a techno-loving journalist from Boston – she's working on a book about Brian Eno.

The glamour of the weekend suddenly reaches its limits later in the evening at Sonar's great fifteenth birthday bash. Sollmann's been booked to play; the club is located outside the city, far beyond the airport. Apart from four English guys, we're the only guests, and it remains that way for the next few hours. It's a mystery why the organisers would have their party start as early as half past eight, especially as the next day is a holiday and the Spanish football team is playing in the semi-final of the European Championship. No one's going to show up before two o'clock on this Sunday morning, but all the clubs will be bursting at the seams by sunrise. This particular club is an open-air disco built in the Pacific-colonial style. Next to it is a stream which flows out to the sea. At some point a terrible stench breaks out – untreated sewage which is released into the stream at the weekend, explains one of the employees. After Sollmann finishes his set it takes a good forty five minutes for the promised taxi to arrive and take us back to the city.

The Sonar weekend is immensely popular with the European party crowd not only because of the festival itself, but also because of the numerous parties which are organised on the fringes of it. Every self-respecting label puts a night on, either in one of the many clubs or by the beach. Whether it's Berlin labels like Mobilee, Innervisions, Bpitch, m_nus and Gigolo or the Kompakt crew from Cologne – they all put in an appearance and they all want to showcase their talent. It's as if someone had taken the principal cast of a clubbing weekend in Berlin and strewn it over Barcelona. This can seem odd at times. Not quite as bizarre as at the Nuits Sonores festival in Lyon in May 2008, where the site's three warehouse venues were called

'Prenzlauer Berg', 'Kreuzberg' and 'Alexanderplatz', the toilets were the 'Spree', and the VIP area was 'Panoramabar' – but it's not far off. The keyword **glocalisation** has already cropped up in this book. It describes the phenomenon of a world which has been flattened and covered over with a virtual network so that scenesters from any place can participate both in their local reality and in a globally accessible yet authentically local subculture somewhere on the other side of the world. At Sonar, you can experience this local culture on tour at one of the hotspots of its global proliferation.

We're driven to the swimming pool by the sea which Kompakt has hired for its party. The water has been drained out of the main pool and this is where the sound system has been set up. Dial owes a great deal to Kompakt; its records are distributed via Cologne, and Philipp Sollmann is waved through at the door without any questions when he says 'guestlist' and holds up his record case. An American girl laughs and says, 'Looking German surely helps a lot.'

This weekend functions like a giant barometer of what's hot right now. Yes, you could see all these artists within a few months if you stayed in Berlin, too, but not spread over a manageable programme of three days, and not via the club network of a city which is happy to offer itself as a temporary stage for this contest. 'Was it good? Who played? Was it full? Did you stay for long? Where did you go afterwards?' Everyone knows each another, everyone's spending a weekend checking out the rest of the field. We go back to the hotel at around half past three.

On the plane back to Berlin the next day a good third of the seats are occupied by DJs, bookers, label managers and others from the industry. All eyes are bleary, but spirits are high.

Partying until your hair starts to glow: Monday

It's difficult, near impossible, to write about an after-party Monday. The reason is simple: drugs. Everyone knows that night life doesn't function without them, never has and never will. But on Fridays and Saturdays, the classic weekend nights, numerous other things play a role – the music, the conversation, the social setting, sex, fashion – and consequently there are many people who go through the night in relative sobriety, having just a few drinks. Of course, all these other things still exist on Monday mornings, it's just that they've become completely irrelevant. The only reason to still be out at this point is wrapped up in a little paper pouch in the pocket of your jeans. When the contents of the pouch are all gone, you soon realise how exhausted you actually are. And then you go home.

To portray this situation accurately, you'd have to write about the dealers. This isn't the done thing, of course, no one wants anything to happen to them. Most of the people who sell drugs in techno circles are people who love to party and are acting on this conviction. Like bar staff, door staff, sound technicians, glass collectors, bookers and all the others who contribute to a successful club night, they're an integral part of the scene. Like the others, they receive no great accolades, and it's best that way.

It also shouldn't be said of any club that it's a good place to take drugs. All Berlin clubs have tightened their drug checks in recent years; none of them can be said to have lax security. Time and again rumours circulate about plain-clothes police being in regular attendance at clubs, observing people in order to identify dealers before calling in their colleagues to arrest them. Of course, the fact remains that drugs are taken all over the place. Where there's a will, there's a way to the loo.

Techno is a participatory culture: either you throw yourself in at the deep end, or you won't have a lot of fun. Those who come along just to watch miss out on a fundamental part of the experience. Unlike other musical genres, techno has never allowed the concept of the stage show to assert its dominance. Sure, going out clubbing means watching an artist at work – but it's also much more than this. Those who choose to throw themselves in at the deep end often leave their rational minds at the cloakroom, and they do so with pleasure. It's part and parcel of the night-life experience. Of course, you have to collect your rational mind again when you leave. You need it back in order to sort out all the confusion, to put the jumbled impressions of the night together, to establish a narrative.

That's one thing.

The other is that no one wants to do techno any harm. How nice it is that this music is recognised as culture at all! How nice that our national cultural institution, the Goethe Institute, has been flying techno DJs around the world in recent years as ambassadors of the best and most valuable culture this country has to share with the world. 'Just don't write anything about drugs, or people will think techno is just about "bosh, bosh, bosh,"' a colleague said to me whilst I was writing this book, referring to Lützenkirchen's after-hour hit 'Drei Tage Wach' ('Three Days Awake'). 'Well, isn't it?' I answered, only half joking. After all, you can trace the development of this music back to Karl-Heinz Stockhausen; you can talk about Kraftwerk, automation and The Man-Machine; you can describe the complex intercultural exchange between Detroit and Berlin. However, you can also say that a more important factor for this type of music is that every weekend a certain number of people - who may be of any background, level of education, age or gender - are willing to neck a couple of pills and go in search of sounds to enhance their high.

There are certain things which are simply better left in the dark. If you want to know more, you'll find out. If you don't, you won't.

So Mondays are somewhat monothematic; there's not too much to report. Suffice to say that if you fall down a K-hole on a Monday morning; if you're sitting by a snow-speckled glass table in the back room of some club with your eyes closed having your hair cut by a stranger; if you talk and talk and talk and talk about the most intimate things to people you only know by their first names because you've only just met them; if you're indiscriminately necking any last remaining drugs that are going, then that's the one thing left on your mind.

That's Monday.
By Tuesday everyone's finally gone home.

Rave mother, rave daughter
Interviews: Anton Waldt

When it's the mum that goes clubbing and her daughter who gets worried: a discussion about family role reversals.

Kerstin is 39 and has been a raver for seventeen years, with all that this entails. Her daughter Betty is 19. Kerstin now works as a stylist.

Kerstin, what was it that first interested you about the rave lifestyle? The music, or going out and taking drugs?
Going out and taking drugs! I mean, it's not as if I was caning kilos of speed and staying out for five days at a time like Nancy from the Bunker. I only started doing that in the last six or seven years. I used to get home as early as eight or nine in the morning. So I wasn't a drug-addict as a young mother. I was popping pills back then, but that increased over the years. I didn't dive straight in and then keep up the same level for fifteen years.

How is it possible to carry on the clubbing lifestyle indefinitely as a single mum?

It wasn't possible at all when Betty was very little. But when she was about three we lived in a squat and my neighbour was an old friend. She was more of a drinker, and always went home around three or four. That meant I could stay out longer. Besides, our door was always open, and we were sharing a large kitchen; there were often friends there who looked after Betty.

And when did you start staying out until midday?

That was when Betty was maybe five or six. She would get up at nine and have breakfast with my flatmate or make something for herself. I would come home at midday, but when you have a child you don't go to bed when you get back, you play with your child. I pretty much always carried on through without sleeping.

Doesn't your daughter notice that you're totally buzzing?

Yeah. But if you're used to someone acting differently sometimes then it becomes normal again. It was never explicitly made an issue, like, 'Oh God, isn't mummy terrible, coming home mashed again. I feel so guilty, my poor little child …' I was simply tired and wanted to go to sleep. But I never made Betty complicit in what I was doing. She's my daughter and not my best friend who I blab everything to.

Partying is about going beyond boundaries, rules, moderation and so on. Then you go home, and as a mum you set boundaries for your child …

Of course, it's completely skewed! Betty notices that sometimes, too. If I'm in a foul mood on a Monday and I'm trying to tell her what she can or can't do, she might ask, 'Are you on a comedown?' That's when I go to my room and keep my mouth shut. And I think: yeah, you're right. I am. I mean I like to go clubbing, but I also have to work. I do the washing, I do all the housework, and I earn the money.

So your stance is: I've not finished growing up yet either, but I still manage to get a lot done?

Yes, exactly! That's the deal.

How does your daughter react when she notices that things are very different in other families?

It's always been seen as exotic that Betty has such a wild mum. Kids tend to think it's cool: 'Round your house you're allowed to do so and so, brilliant! Your mum's well chilled.' When she turned sixteen and I knew that her friends were starting to smoke weed, I asked her, 'Have you been in contact with drugs?' She knows about them from me anyway, and she's also aware of the drug issue because her father died of an overdose.

When did you explain that to her?

Very early on. I always told her if she asked something. You explain that there are various drugs, what drugs do to your body, the fact that you can get addicted, that some drugs are more dangerous than others, but also that drugs are part of what people choose to do in their free time in our society. I always explained it in a matter-of-fact way, and never said, 'I was out munching pills again last night!'

And if she asks you specifically which party drugs you take? Pills, MDMA, speed?

Then I'd say, 'I take everything.' But Betty's never been under the impression that she's living with a desperate person who needs her help. In any case, she's never asked me outright. And I wouldn't say to my child, 'I've got drug problems, we have to talk.' Ridiculous!

What about taking hard drugs when your child is there?

No!! That's out of the question for me. I know some proper caners who take hard drugs in front of their children. I don't agree with that. Or Martin, whose mum was with the Spiral Tribe. He's the same age as Betty and he'd already started drinking by the time he was six. His mum often left him with me. He liked it at our place because there were toys and he could suddenly be a child again. Otherwise he acted like a grown-up. One time when he was sleeping at our place he asked if he could have a bit of LSD because he couldn't sleep. I was pretty shocked. Another time I met him in a run-down squat pub. Little Martin was sitting there on a bar stool, pissed out of his face, calling for Betty: 'Hey, where's Betty? I really wanna play with Betty!' I often talked to his mum about it. But later they moved away from Berlin again.

So your daughter saw some crazy stuff quite early on.

Yeah. But a butcher's child also grows up watching their dad hack up animals. It doesn't mean the child will be traumatised and turn into a mass murderer. And it's not just my raving that Betty knows about. I mean, I also had quite a colourful love life! Betty has been confronted with my hedonism in its entirety. For Betty, it was always perfectly normal that there are men who love other men, because she learned about it when she was younger. From a neighbour of ours, for instance, who often came to baby sit. The other thing is that she's growing up in a big city where you often come across the most bizarre people. I mean, we live in Berlin and not a little town in western Germany. Sometimes half of the parents are stoned at the school parents' evening: hippies, East-German-Nazi-rave-skinheads whose son is called Attila or whatever. But I've never been one of those committed parents who bake cakes at the weekends or help renovate the school … I couldn't be bothered with that. Of course, sometimes I think that was rubbish on my part. But would Betty have been any better off if I'd have done that kind of thing?

Don't parents normally try to set a good example?

Yes, but perhaps it's also good to set a bad example for your child sometimes. Because then they'll have no desire to go off the rails in the same way. When Betty's friends smoke weed she knows precisely how stupid it is because she's seen her mum when she's stoned. Since she turned fifteen she's been telling me that weed makes you stupid. Yep! Sorry, you're right!

Does your child already know better than you?

No, my daughter is my equal. She has the right, and my permission, to judge my behaviour.

Would you seriously call yourself a bad mother?

Of course. Because there are lots of things I didn't do just because they were inconvenient. But I think that my mum would think of herself just as badly. It's surely normal to criticise yourself.

You mean that mothers criticise themselves anyway, so there's no great need to hide anything from your child?

Exactly! That's my basic theory. Later she'll tell me what things were shit for her anyway. So why should I put up a pretence? I can be shit in the first place, but honestly at least. With our parents there was such an incredible number of rules, and you quickly realised that they were unnecessary, ridiculous and stupid.

Whether you go raving and don't tell the child, or whether you do it openly and then hope that she won't make the same mistakes – aren't these the same double standards?

Sure. But aren't there always some double standards at work?

Do you know any other rave mothers?

Yeah, you always come across some. But most of them have had their children later. When I see what an act they put on: 'I just can't do it if my child's there,' that kind of thing. I wouldn't have had any qualms myself; I've brought Betty with me to open-air parties. One friend of mine always tells her eight-year-old son she's going to work. Although sometimes she really is working on the bar for the night.

Do you quickly make it obvious to your fellow ravers that you're a mother?

It's not something that you shout from the rooftops. Most clubbing friendships are superficial anyway – kisses on the cheek, small talk: 'Were you at that party? Did you see so and so?' And then, 'See you later!' I know a huge number of people just from clubbing who I wouldn't allow into my daily life. I really can't be bothered with people who are so muddled and hazy. I can hang around with them at the weekend when I'm just as high as they are. During the week, when I'm functioning, it's a completely different story. I really don't want them coming round to chill; that kind of thing gets on my wick. For me, Sunday evening is the end of it. Then it starts again on Friday evening. There are people who just don't get that. They go on to the next after-party and so on … I rarely join in with all that, partly because I have a child. I'm aware of my responsibility; it keeps me grounded – if I didn't have my daughter I'd be getting wrecked on a whole other level. And because I've had her, I've always kept at least one wheel on the track.

When she moves out, will that be the end for you?

Yes, exactly! She'll probably end up visiting her sixty-year-old, morphine-addicted mother in an old people's home, bringing her a package every now and then: 'You got anything on you? Come on, hand it over, your mum needs it. Come on Betty, sort me out with something!' Then she'll say, 'Haven't you had enough already?'

Kerstin's daughter Betty was a year and a half old when her father died of a heroin overdose. Then Kerstin moved with her to Berlin, living in a squat at first. Betty's currently doing an apprenticeship.

My mum's a raver! Is that something you'd say, Betty?

I'd say my mum goes clubbing a lot. And I mean a lot! As far back as I can remember. When I was very little – before I started school – I was very clingy. When I realised during the night that my mum wasn't there I sometimes woke the whole house up screaming. But I was never completely alone. There was always someone there, like our flatmate, to calm me down. And then the next day my mum would be back again – even if she did sleep for the whole day afterwards!

Did your mum's juvenile behaviour bother you?

When I was young I used to get fed up with it. But it was no huge drama, and eventually I got used to it.

And when did you realise what kind of circles Kerstin was moving in?

Quite early on. Then properly when I was ten and she had a mobile. You could hear a bit of the party going on and Kerstin would shout that she couldn't hear so well ... Then she'd say something like, 'I'll be home in an hour!' Still, sometimes three hours would go by and she wouldn't be back yet. Then she'd say, 'Yeah, I got stuck talking to someone.' That was crap for me sometimes. Or when I couldn't get hold of her at all because her mobile was in the cloakroom. Then I did get worried and I would stay awake until she got home.

A reversal of the classic situation?

Yeah. I prefer to stay in with friends or to come home relatively early if I do go out.

In the normal scenario the child sometimes gets grounded by the mother.

But I couldn't really do that with my mum. And she wouldn't have stuck to it either. So I said, 'Get in touch once a day so I know everything's okay.'

How did you come to realise that other mums don't spend so much time partying?

In my first year at school I told some friends where we live. After that their parents told them they weren't allowed to speak to me: 'Her mum's a squatter and a raver, a very bad influence!' That was really hurtful. There was a gap of four years before my best friend was allowed to play with me again. I only rarely got to go round to her house. She always came to ours, and she thought it was brilliant that my mum wasn't like hers, that she was more chilled. And she loved the fact that Kerstin went clubbing so much. When I was about ten, she was considered really, really cool amongst my friends: 'She's not a square like my mum!' She was the role model back then, and that's actually still the case now.

Isn't it important to feel normal at that age?

Yeah, that was a big issue for me. I was a proper goody-goody two shoes: 'Don't steal! Smoking is evil! You're not allowed to do this, that and the other! If you do that I won't speak to you any more!'

Didn't you ever say that it pissed you off when your friends weren't allowed to play with you? Or ask if you could please move into a normal apartment and for Kerstin to stop all her nonsense?

I can well imagine that I did, but I don't remember. In any case, we moved house when I was in third year. Besides, I was a shy, sweet, good little girl who would never hurt a fly.

Was the 'shy, sweet, good little girl' a reaction to your mother?

To an extent. I've always tried to live a more regular life. But I was still one of the freaks with the wild imaginations in the first few years of school. Later, when I was ten, I was really popular. But at high school I too plain for the cool kids. My mum was so out there and such a party animal, and that's why I never really got into music, for example. Because my mum had so much to do with parties and music. The same goes for fashion and parties, and I didn't touch a drop of alcohol for a long time.

Was this a conscious reaction?

Not necessarily. I thought the fact that Kerstin was so into clothes was a bit over the top. Then when fashion became an important topic for my friends, I said, 'I know about that from home already, I'm not interested.' There are a few specific things that I still can't stand the sight of: I hate camouflage! Later, when I was at high school, people asked you what your name was, and the second question was whether you smoked. That was shit for me, because right from when I was little I had to live with everywhere being so smoky. I often used to get headaches from it.

So did your mother's example put you off?

Yes, and that applies to alcohol too. When she used to get home from a party pissed again and go straight to the bathroom to be sick. Sometimes it was really bad; she'd be sick and then just lie in bed. That was pretty shit for me. I don't even know why people have to drink alcohol. To have more fun? Then the next day you feel ill and maybe you can't even remember the night before. What's the point?

Don't teenagers think it's really cool to get pissed at first? Did this make you an outsider?

Yeah. We're a bit different; we see it as uncool. Whatever you think is cool, we think it's uncool. That's how it was. And then there's the addiction. My mum always says she wants to be independent. But then she smokes like a chimney and drinks – that's being dependent!

Have you ever cited your mother as a bad example at school?

Nah. I've said that people only do things because they're following the crowd, that kind of thing. That's enough to make most people think twice. And my closest friends have never been smokers or drinkers.

But now you have a little tipple from time to time?

Yes. I even got wasted once. I was lovesick and a friend of mine had some wine, which I don't even like to be honest. But at the end of the day it's not even fun. You certainly shouldn't drink so much that you just end up being sick. As long as it stays within certain limits and you don't get off your face, it's OK.

A classic mum comment!

Yeah, great! I also think smoking weed is really stupid. With some people you hardly notice anything, but with others it dulls their minds and they just laugh at everything. It's sad. If that happens to my friends, they get a sermon from me right away.

And your mum?

Well I noticed the difference between joints and cigarettes when I was still in kindergarten, by the smell and by the chat that went with it – adults always think that children don't pick up on these things! I've even broached the subject with friends of my mum: 'Hey, here you are stoned again!' But I can never give my mum a sermon, it wouldn't achieve anything at all. Although it still really bugs me, even now, when I've got friends round and the heart-shaped packet with the stash is lying in the kitchen. Some people still think that's cool.

And other drugs?

Even worse! I mean, my dad gave himself an overdose. I found that out when I was very young. When I was thirteen I knew what drug it was as well. But that's not really important. I know that he died; I know that it was a drug; I know that it wasn't good. That's enough. Otherwise I'd have been too worried about my mum: 'My dad took heroin, what about her?' There's still a bit of that now. She should do what she wants; as long as nothing happens it's okay.

Do you have any interest in electronic music?

Although I prefer the electric guitar, I've started to quite like most of the stuff my mum plays. But once when I was still in kindergarten my mum took me with her to the Love Parade. I hated it and cried the whole time!

You're only nineteen, perhaps you'll still get a taste for it?

Staying up all night is okay, talking with friends or whatever, but partying in clubs? I really don't feel the need. My mum's done enough partying for the both of us, and probably for my children too – if I have any. I prefer going to concerts, and at the moment my friends and I play Warhammer, a role playing game. This actually winds my mum up: 'Help, my daughter's a Trekkie!'

Do you think your mum will ever cut down on clubbing?

I wouldn't be so sure. She's kept it up this far, to the age of 39, so why not carry on? Even if she sometimes feels funny because she's one of the older ones at the club. I think 'acting your age' is stupid anyway. If it suits you and you're having fun then you should just do it – as long you can still get in!

Have you ever wished your mum was completely average?

Sometimes I've wished she was at home more often. But basically I think my mum's great as she is. A bit loopy too. I think it's amazing that she manages to do so much: excessive partying, excessive working, and then fitting in the housework, and those times where she just lies in bed. She takes everything to the extreme.

Has this made you particularly independent?

Yes. When she's away, let's say for two weeks because of a job, I manage to look after the household quite well, and I'm good at looking after money. Oh yeah, and there aren't any parties thrown at my place!

The great techno assembly kit

From Berghain to American churches: the incredible story of the music software Ableton Live

A classic record shop scenario: two or three DJs and producers are standing at the counter going through the new records and one says, yeah, he quite likes this tune, but he really couldn't play it. It's constructed too simply; someone's just used this and that effect and then stuck it through a certain filter. And sooner or later the name of a Berlin software firm and its sole product always crops up: Ableton Live, a programme for producing music.

These conversations are a daily occurrence. It's become very easy to produce techno and house. Almost every DJ makes their own music nowadays, whereas in the nineties DJing and producing were two clearly distinct spheres. Back then hardly anyone used to play live in a club, either. It was far too arduous to set up all the synthesisers, sequencers, drum machines and other instruments. This is no longer necessary. The instruments have all migrated into the computer, so artists can play from their laptops.

It wouldn't have been this way without Ableton Live. If the long-running children's TV series 'Die Sendung mit der Maus'

('Mouse TV') did a feature on how music gets from a computer to a speaker, it would surely start like this: 'This is Robert. Robert has made a programme which allows you to play music on a computer. Everyone wants to have the programme. Robert is going to show us how it works, because Robert is also a musician.' The Robert in question is Robert Henke, one half of the techno act Monolake and co-developer of Live.

Artist, engineer, philosopher, fanatic

Asked about what he's done for Ableton, Henke plays down his role: 'This isn't my product at all,' he says. 'I'm just one of the people involved. Sure, I have an important position. But there are now a hundred people working for Ableton. All decisions are made by the team.'

Henke is an interesting guy. He's tall, slim and strong. Sometimes he has short hair, but most of the time his head is shaved. In the mid-nineties he liked to go around wearing black leathers; now he wears a shirt and trousers, but he still has his piercings from back then (one of his first records was called 'Piercing Music'). He gives off that pleasant mixture of boyishness and confidence which you often encounter with nerds whose passion for technical detail hasn't robbed them of the art or the pleasure of conversation. Nevertheless, you can still never quite figure him out when you speak to him, and this may have something to do with the fact that he's half a dozen characters rolled into one: a musician, an engineer, a cultural critic, an interface philosopher, a media democrat, a techno fanatic.

We meet at a café on Paul-Linke-Ufer in Kreuzberg, a few doors down from Hardwax, the long-established and extremely influential techno record shop. Henke has just met Torsten Pröfrock, the other half of Monolake, who also releases solo records under the name T++ and who works as a purchaser for Hardwax. As for Henke, in the mid-nineties he worked for the mastering studio Dubplates & Mastering which is affiliated with Hardwax. Even now, every self-respecting techno and house producer comes here to have the dubplates made which are used for the final pressing. Countless vinyl records have the initials 'D & M' printed after the lead-out groove. And the first Monolake records were released on Chain Reaction, one of the labels founded on the fringes of the record shop.

Henke comes from Munich, and you can just about detect his Bavarian intonation. He grew up in a family of engineers, and he too was meant to become an engineer, he says, until his interest in electronic music got in the way. When he was still at school he bought himself a simple synthesiser and began playing around with it. He was the keyboard player in a band at school, and at home he made sound collages. Then he moved to Berlin.

As for many people who came to Berlin in the late eighties and early nineties, Henke's first night at the newly opened Tresor was a formative influence. 'In was an indescribable experience, how loud, how solid, how raw and at the same time how euphoric it was,' he says with undiminished enthusiasm. He was actually enrolled in computer studies and communication studies at Berlin's Technical University, but he soon turned his attention to academic computer music at the university's studio for electronic music.

Techno at one end, academic computer music at the other: these are the two extremes of the spectrum that Henke's work has occupied ever since. At the time the two things went hand in hand quite naturally. Indeed, the furore with which the great boom-boom-boom of techno declared itself the zero-hour of music and aimed to wash away all the old, outdated and superfluous forms not only paved the way for the commercial triumph which was to draw hundreds of thousands of ravers to the Love Parade a few years later. For many people this music also raised questions not dissimilar to those being wrestled with in academic computer music for some time: What sound follows another sound, and why? What does the realm beyond classical tonality sound like? How might one imagine a kind of music consisting of sounds rather than notes? When you feel like you're part of a musical revolution, it makes sense to look to other vanguards as potential allies. Henke got to know Gerhard Behles, who was teaching at the TU, and the two of them began making, releasing and performing music under the name Monolake.

In recent years, Henke and Behles have remastered a few of their old records and rereleased them, and you can hear that they've aged well. This can't be said of too many records produced in the mid-nineties in that grey area between club music and sound research. The fact that a new genre was being created at this time, a genre which was still defining its rules and thus offered a huge range of possibilities, opened up additional room for all kinds of exciting gurgles, hisses, bleeps and bloops. Often it was merely a case of connecting up a few modules and seeing what came of it. It was great, if you were there. Looking back though, it wasn't always as groundbreaking as people assumed at the time.

One of the exceptions was Monolake. The music on their first two albums, **Interstate** and **Hongkong,** has lost none of its grey, shimmering clarity over the years. You can hear that they have their roots in the Basic Channel school of dub techno, although their kick drum doesn't pump along with the same peaceful warmth as on the Basic Channel records. But Monolake can also enter an entirely different mode; 'Plumbicon', for instance, is an absolutely classic main-floor techno track.

He just wants to play

The music is one thing. Even more astounding, however, is the software which was born out of it: Live, a programme which started life as a sequencer designed by Behles and Henke for their own use. In 1999 they founded the Ableton company to continue to develop and market the software. Live first came onto the market in 2001, and each subsequent year a new version has been released. In order to devote his time to the company, Gerhard Behles gradually stopped working with Monolake. Since 2003, Henke has been continuing the Monolake project with Torsten Pröfrock.

From the very beginning, Henke says, Live was intended as a programme which could be used for precisely that: playing live. 'The previous paradigm was for music to be composed on the computer. That meant doing something, then pressing Play, then listening to it, thinking about it, changing something and pressing Play again. With Live it suddenly became possible to do all of this without having to keep pressing Stop. You could change things as it was playing. This is its recipe for success. It's just fun to use. Musical ideas often have a short lifespan. They surface and then vanish again. Software that's intuitive to use will always have an advantage over a very complex programme.'

The way Ableton has revolutionised making music on a computer is similar to what Photoshop has done for image editing. Previously, programmes for making music were in the studio software category. They weren't designed to be played around with. They were tools for recording and editing music. With Ableton Live, the software has become an actual musical instrument.

A little philosophical tangent: who actually makes techno?

Almost all of the music we listen to today is electronic, Brian Eno once said. And he's right, of course. We even listen to the calls of humpback whales through a CD player. However, whether it's a symphony orchestra, a jazz ensemble or a rock band that you're listening to on the kitchen radio – you immediately know that it's a case of musicians playing instruments and these sounds being recorded and mixed. In electronic music, it's far less simple. Who actually makes techno: a musician, a producer or a computer? Electronic music has a plausibility problem: even when laptop artists are performing live, there's no way of visually following what you can hear.

Indeed, most artists who make electronic music also consider themselves producers rather than musicians. This is the result of a long process in music history. In the beginning, a producer was simply the person who pressed the record button when the musicians started playing. In principle the producer's role hasn't changed – it's just that all those people who used to play the music have disappeared. From the eighties onwards, they've been replaced by all manner of machines, and even these machines have now become redundant. Synthesisers and sequencers have been digitally replicated and installed on computers, as have all kinds of string sounds, every imaginable drum kit and dozens of effects such as filters, reverb and distortion.

But where there's no drummer and no bassist on hand, drums and bass have to be programmed. The track has to be given an arrangement. This involves a great deal of planning and consideration, but music will always thrive on spontaneous ideas as well. Ideally, then, it should always remain possible to alter a part of a track while it's already playing. This is the role of the producer. The producer makes techno. In theoretical terms, you might call this a complex authorial position.

The Lego bricks of music

Electronic dance music basically follows a modular architecture. The smallest musical unit is the loop, which is made up of several sounds and can be repeated indefinitely. On its own, a loop is normally quite unremarkable and replaceable, but in combination with other loops it creates the segments of four or eight bars which make up a track. Meanwhile, the tracks themselves also function as modules when a DJ threads them together into a set.

There has never been a detailed study of how this modular structure came to be. An explanation rooted in technology might start with the mechanisation of rhythm in the late seventies before pointing to the development of the MIDI protocol which taught music machines to communicate with one another. An account based on music history would surely begin with the first remixes, which were disco tracks extended using a reel-to-reel tape deck. DJs would re-record a passage which worked well on the dance floor and paste it in the desired position – this is called editing, and it's still practised today. Using a computer, however, a job which might have lasted days back then can be completed in minutes. This is how the loop found its way into dance music – in the literal sense, as these were actual loops of audio tape which repeated certain rhythm passages. The first Detroit techno tracks were also created using this traditional copy-and-paste method – and these tracks demonstrate another root of the modular principle, one which had great repercussions: if you look at the way different features of composition developed, disco and funk were still oriented towards the song principle, with the verse and the chorus as their main structural features. House and techno tracks, on the other hand, are built up using loops and modules.

This sounds more complicated than it is. Once you've seen the interface of Ableton Live, you immediately understand what it's all about. One view is called the 'arrangement'. When you click this view, you see a long row of coloured rectangles, called 'clips'. These are arranged along a time axis. They look like Lego bricks and each one represents a piece of musical material: a drum sound, a keyboard sample, a bassline. When they're put together in an arrangement, they make up a track. In principle, it's as if you had the drum machine, the keyboard and the bass synthesiser plugged in directly and you were having them play all at the same time. This can also be visualised in a different way. This is called the 'session' view and it looks like a classic studio mixing desk. Each audio channel has its own controls which can be used to manipulate the clips. The clips are constructed by putting together various samples; then they can be drag-and-dropped to the arrangement. An experienced producer can read the arrangement like a classical musician reads a musical score.

However, this is not what has made Ableton Live such a global success. Other programmes function in exactly the same way. This architecture merely transposes the old studio set-up of the analogue world into the computer – although Ableton offers a particularly simple overview because everything takes place within one window and you don't have to deal with various pop-ups. The key feature of this software, however, is that it allows you to edit individual samples in real time. This means that you can take individual modules out, alter them and insert them back into the mix whilst the track is playing.

The samples can be reversed, trimmed down, sped up, duplicated, stretched, chopped up and rearranged clearly, simply and without any great loss of sound quality. A myriad of filters can be used to achieve all kinds of effects – you can find the entire sound palette of techno and house here in a few dozen effects. The way you control the whole operation is a matter of personal taste. For some, a computer and a mouse are sufficient. Others feel more at home when they have real knobs to turn. Robert Henke has had his own control surface built, the 'Monodeck'.

The process, then, is quite simple: you take a beat from the huge beat library, a bass sound from the huge bass library and a keyboard line from the huge keyboard library, drag them into the arrangement window and arrange them with one another. Hey presto, you've got a simple rhythm track. Then, with a bit of practice, you can apply infinite variations to it: if you want your bass to sound like it comes from a mid-nineties dub techno track, you can even find the typical Basic Channel resonator. This is named 'Berlin', and is located in the resonators folder alongside 'Brooklyn', 'Moscow', and the more extreme 'Valhalla'.

In fact, you can even imagine Ableton Live as someone having transferred around twenty-five years of techno and house history into the eternal present of a simple computer interface. And it's not only the flow of sound that you can continually remould, as if it were a clay model extending into time instead of space – the programme itself is basically a large sculpture, an organism which continually regenerates itself through automatic updates. It's both the culmination of a long tradition of dance music and an instrument for shaping this music's future.

Like a Swiss Army knife

Ableton makes you think well beyond the limits of house and techno. If all music is computer music, that means everyone can use Live. For instance, you could feed the entire sound library of a symphony orchestra into Ableton Live to use as an add-on. Indeed, the programme has long-since been discovered by users who aren't making techno or house. Musicians, producers and composers from every possible genre have appropriated it as a musical notebook which they can carry around on their laptop. What started as the software of a techno duo in the mid-nineties has become the core of an extremely successful company. Over a hundred people work for Ableton, and a few years ago the company founded a branch in New York.

The headquarters in Berlin is located on two elongated floors of a renovated old factory building near Rosa Luxemburg Platz in Mitte. They've just expanded the premises, and some rooms are still being refitted. The reception area is businesslike and without frills. In front of the large, white Ableton logo on a green background, which used to be right by the entrance, is now simply the programming department. It's tidy, bright, spacious, and in the corner – like an ironic reminder of the founding period – there's actually a table football table. They also have a shared dining room. It's how you'd imagine a grown-up technology start-up – New Economy which has outlasted the hype and the crash.

A good half of the hundred staff work in the development department. The others are responsible for marketing, accounts, sales or technical support. The latter probably know Ableton Live about as well as anyone besides Robert Henke himself. Their job is to answer calls from people who are working with Live and are having difficulties for one reason or another. And this user base went beyond just techno producers long ago.

'Ableton Live is like a Swiss Army knife. People use it for things which we'd never have thought of,' explains Dominik Wilms, head of the technical support department. 'In the USA, many church services are now conducted with the help of Live. For churches which don't have a backing band there are now firms which offer Live sets for church services, broken down into individual tracks. It's really bizarre: if you watch a little video of one of these services, you see someone with a Powerbook, an audio interface and a MIDI controller next to the altar – the same set-up you might see in the DJ booth at Berghain.' And the producer who makes the music for the American quiz show 'Jeopardy' – she's an Ableton Live user too. So is the industrial rocker Trent Reznor; and the film music composer Hans Zimmer, winner of numerous Oscars, Grammys and Golden Globes; and some of the pop producers who manufacture music for superstars like Kylie Minogue. The software created in the mid-nineties because Robert Henke and Gerhard Behles needed a sequencer has evolved into a programme used all over the world for all kinds of purposes.

Certainly the majority of techno producers are now working with Live. Wilms says he always gets a shock when one of his heroes is on the phone. He's in his mid-thirties and comes from Krefeld, where he used to organise and DJ at house nights. He studied information technology and worked for a sound card manufacturer before joining Ableton.

Most of Ableton's employees have a similar background. Many come from the techno scene. Nico Starke, who also works in technical support, is one of them. He was a Tresor resident for a long time under the alias Dry, and he used to manage the club's website during the week. But after he got the job at Ableton he didn't DJ as much, he says. Eventually he gave up his residency altogether.

It's not the best subject to dwell on, but working for a firm like Ableton is also an opportunity to remain part of the techno scene when you're no longer able or willing to party the whole time. And Ableton is not the only large music software firm in Berlin to be born out of the techno scene. The other is Native Instruments. It produces Traktor Scratch, a programme which allows DJs to simulate vinyl DJing on a computer. Its staff also includes some retired DJs.

Can a programme be too simple?

'It's very simple to make a track that sounds good using Live,' says Benjamin Weiss when asked his opinion of the software. Weiss is a producer himself, under the alias Nerk and as one half of the duo Toktok, and he works as a music technology editor for the magazine De:Bug. 'However, this is both a blessing and a curse for the programme, as most people are content to get that far. Only very few take things a step further.'

In actual fact, says Weiss, people should avoid using the sounds which are included with the programme. They could record the sound of their toaster instead, or manipulate a sine wave until it produces a noise which was never there to begin with and which can then be arranged in the most unlikely patterns along the time axis.

Robert Henke also sometimes gets annoyed about the number of tracks which all sound the same. This is not because he feels indirectly responsible for it. Rather his dismay stems from a basic cultural criticism of the way people shamelessly think they have to post their music on MySpace. Nevertheless, not far from the cultural critic in Henke lurks a media democrat: 'If everyone had Live,' he says, 'then it would be much easier for everyone to judge whether a piece of music is actually exciting or not. Just like everyone who's ever tried to take a photo has a feeling for how good a picture is. Music software has yet to reach the same level of familiarity as a digital camera or a pencil, but we're definitely on the right track. At that point everyone will be able to cobble something together from ready-made components, and no one will think of calling it music any more. No one will still regard the tracks someone makes when they get home from work in the same light as the work of a producer who has spent half their life studying how to make music. And the more the instrument begins to resemble a pencil, the more ridiculous it will seem to have a conversation about what exactly – what pencil – you're using.' In a certain respect, Ableton has succeeded in building the ultimate music machine, the device which knows no boundaries, at least for the time being.

However, this also complicates the aesthetic upheaval, contradicts the eternal desire to start afresh which many artists have inherited from the twentieth century and brought into the present – including Henke. The great, all-encompassing revolution, says Henke, has taken place in the shadows over the past few years. 'Electronic music was always music versus technology, music which tried to push the limits of what technology could achieve. This has ceased to be the case. In recent years, the technology has reached a point where the technical possibilities far exceed the skills of its users.' Henke says he personally uses nothing but Ableton Live for making music. 'But even if I were to spend every hour of every day for the rest of my life making music, just using this programme, I wouldn't come up against any limits. This is a major revolution.'

This presents another answer to the question as to who actually makes techno. With this programme, you are simultaneously a composer, an arranger, a conductor, a sound engineer and an all-round musician. You slip into the various musical roles just like you do with the players in a Playstation football game: you're always the one who's currently on the ball. The others are controlled by the programme – via the parameters which you define yourself.

We sell taste

How do you run a successful label when fewer and fewer people are buying records?

It's a paradox. The vinyl record survived a good twenty years longer because dance music didn't want to give it up as a medium. Techno and house on one hand, and hip hop on the other, were genres where the DJs determined which format would be used. In the meantime, the music industry has collapsed and seen a slump in turnover of almost 50 percent. And now? Although the vinyl record is seeing a quite remarkable comeback – almost every music shop now has a vinyl section again, and even the consumer electronics giant Media Markt sells the latest indie releases as records – more and more DJs are giving up playing vinyl. Instead they are using their laptops and programmes like Traktor Scratch which allow them to mix their digital tracks. The question as to whether this entails a loss of sound quality is still being debated, but this doesn't change the fact that an ever greater number of DJs are leaving their records at home.

Of course, the vinyl market was and still is a niche market. As remarkable as the growth in LP sales is, their proportion in relation to the music sold on all formats remains well under one percent. And sales of 12" singles, the most important physical format for electronic dance music, rarely exceeded a few thousand units even when business was good. These times are now gone.

'A record which would previously have sold 5,000 units only reaches around 2,000 sales now,' says Steffen Berkhahn, better known by his DJ alias Dixon. Berkhahn, too, has been DJing primarily with CDs for some time now.

As Dixon he is known as a prominent Berlin house DJ and as co-manager of Innervisions, one of Berlin's most successful new record labels of recent years. But how do you run a record label when fewer and fewer people are buying records, Mr Berkhahn?

The first surprise is that just because vinyl records aren't selling as well as before, it doesn't mean there are less labels around, or even less releases. Berkhahn states right away that releasing music is easier nowadays, at least in theory. It's easier to gain access to the market. Why? Because it's impossible for downloads to be left on the shelf. The principle is quite simple. If you've made a piece of music, you set up a net label and put the track up for sale through online sales platforms. Even if no one buys it, you've not made a loss. This wasn't always the case. Previously you had to start by investing in an initial pressing, and if this went badly the records would eventually be returned and your money would be lost. Nowadays, Berkhahn explains, if net label managers see that a download is popular, they can still get a small record pressing done, safe in the knowledge that they'll be likely to shift all the copies. So that's how things stand, and as a result, there are huge numbers of new releases.

Innervisions

Steffen Berkhahn suggests doing the interview at his home, an apartment in an attractive old building in Prenzlauer Berg. It's May 2008. A few days ago he had a very unfortunate bicycle accident and injured his shoulder. He's unable to use his right arm for a few weeks and has had to cancel a tour of Japan. The DJ in his slippers, an interesting insight when you're used to seeing the stylish Dixon out in clubs. Sitting at the kitchen table, he describes the rules by which a record label can still be run today.

First, a label has to be a filter. Dixon puts it a nicer way: a label has to consistently deliver quality. The labels' previous calculation, whereby they simply had to release lots of records and hope that a couple of big hits would carry the costs of the duds, no longer applies. Second, a label needs a face. The personality of the people running the label must be evident in everything the label does. This means going out and playing records, and this is the third rule in any case, as the label can no longer earn a profit just by selling records. The records increase the label's prominence – and this is important when it comes to setting performance fees. And last but not least, it's essential to pay attention to marketing, and to set your label up as a publisher in order to sell the rights to the music.

Dixon is a veteran of Berlin night life. He's been DJing since the early nineties. He actually wanted to become a professional sportsman, but an injury threw his career off the rails, and when he discovered the exploding club scene of the post-reunification period he soon forgot about his physiotherapy. He's also a true believer. It may have been Alex Empire's raucous Bass Terror parties which attracted him to Berlin's night life at first, but even back then he was DJing house. This wasn't always easy in a city like Berlin which is more inclined towards faster, rougher techno beats.

He doesn't run Innervisions alone. His partners are Kristian Beyer and Frank Wiedemann. They both come from Karlsruhe, and they are the label's most successful act under the alias Âme. Innervisions started out as part of Sonar Kollektiv, the sprawling label collective based around the group Jazzanova. When Innervisions released its seventh record it made itself independent, but it continued in the same vein, releasing a successful mix of different house interpretations. The tracks included the wonderful, slow piano piece 'Blade Dancer' by Tokyo Black Star; the bleak, driving 'Where We At' by Henrik Schwarz, Dixon and Âme; Âme's tech-house bomb 'Rej', which is the label's biggest hit with 28,000 copies sold; and 'Back To My Roots' by Laurent Garnier, the come-back record of the Frenchman who'd been lurking in the shadow of his own huge name for several years and rediscovered his old form for Innervisions.

Indeed, the example of Garnier says a lot about the functioning of these networks which are so vital for a label's success. Garnier and Dixon were playing together at Panoramabar, Garnier played a track, Dixon asked excitedly what it was, Garnier said it was something new, Dixon asked if he could release it, Garnier said yes. A few days later a message arrived to confirm the arrangement. 'I've never released a track by someone I don't know,' says Berkhahn. 'It all happens via networks. And if I don't know someone personally then it's someone who's been recommended by people I trust. It's a network which spans the whole world. Sending off demos is a waste of time. The crazy undiscovered artist who tinkers around in their basement and reinvents house – there's no such thing.'

Almost all successful new labels of recent years are based on these kinds of networks – whether it's Mobilee, Vakant, m_nus or Innervisions. The people involved have known each other for years, they trust one another, and they've also seen their style go through the doldrums for a while without letting themselves get discouraged. A label is a central point in such a network, but not the only one. Regular club nights with a guestlist for contacts are another. Dixon, for instance, organised the monthly Innercity night at Weekend for a long time. After a break it switched in autumn 2008 to the newly opened club Violet. Then there are the record shops. Kristian Beyer runs Plattentasche in Karlsruhe; Marcus Worgull, a DJ from Wuppertal who's released two records on Innervisions, co-owns Groove Attack in Cologne.

It's impossible to overestimate the importance of record shops in the evolution of dance music. In most cases where an exciting new scene has developed somewhere, a record shop has been at the centre of things. But today, they also act as a gauge of people's declining interest in vinyl records. You can see this in the age distribution of their customers. 'No one is coming up to join the ranks,' says Berkhahn. 'Young people buy digital. End of story.'

However, he doesn't subscribe to the view that this entails the disappearance of a culture. For one thing, he mostly DJs with CDs himself, and secondly, digital formats also present commercial advantages. You can reach customers who wouldn't have bought from you before, he says. Not only because they don't buy records any more or don't live near a record shop. 'When we released a double EP with eight tracks, the most successful track hit two thousand downloads. The least successful was downloaded fifty times, so it had some fans too. But many of those who only downloaded one or two tracks may not have bought the entire double EP at all.' This is income which would have been lost without the digital format.

A label which releases four records a year can never support its managers and half a dozen artists, regardless of whether the music is available on analogue or digital formats. But then, it doesn't have to. The label functions precisely because the people running it don't make their living from it. All in all, it brings in enough money to pay the salary of one person who looks after the day-to-day running of the label. This person gets a salary. Any money left over is immediately put back into the company.

You can see this when you look at the records. 'The object we're selling has to be a good object,' says Dixon. That means expensive covers which are not only printed in four colours but also covered with a special coating. The graphic designer Pierre Becker has come up with an instantly recognisable style of artwork for Innervisions which makes striking changes with each design, but always incorporates the same basic elements. Another extra cost is using thick pieces of vinyl. Then there's the matter of keeping the number of releases down. 'The records have to have time to breathe,' reasons Dixon. Labels whose releases follow hot on each other's heels can make their records look old very quickly. 'It's not just about the music. Anyone who thinks so is mistaken. If that were the case, people would only download their music nowadays.'

DJ gigs are the handbags of the music business

You could express it as a formula: record label minus records equals label. A brand. Indeed, the comparison with a major fashion designer is not so far-fetched. The main reason they maintain their haute couture ranges is to nurture their brand image, whilst the money is made on the prêt-à-porter ranges and accessories. Record labels are heading down a similar path: the vinyl records are the equivalent of the haute couture dresses. They too are intended to give off an ever-greater aura of handcraft and unite other brand attributes. Sentences such as 'That was real fashion back then' or 'No one would actually wear that on the street' are almost the exact equivalent of statements like 'All the best tracks have already been made' and 'Record cases are too heavy'. Meanwhile, the larger music market is catered for with downloads. These are comparable with the prêt-à-porter ranges, and whilst the fashion labels have counterfeit goods to contend with, the record labels are concerned about illegal downloads. The real money, though, is made from playing gigs – which might therefore be called the handbags of the music business.

However, there's something else which is even more important: every successful label is first and foremost an agency for cultivating taste. To succeed in this, it's not enough to have good taste, you also need the will to assert it. This requires both a sense of timing and a good dose of confidence.

Dixon is someone who has these qualities. If he throws on a scarf, a few months later everyone's walking down Kastanienallee wearing one. Although Dixon only wears his when it's cold. If he wants to open a coffee shop, even though he has absolutely no experience in the business, he does it. And just because he's notched up a great success with his mix CD **Body Language Vol. 4**, it doesn't mean that he's going to follow it up immediately with another mix CD. In spite of all the offers. Simply put, if you've been playing to a dance floor somewhere or other in the western world almost every weekend for the past fifteen years, you know where you're at. This is the message the label has to get across. Then it will be able to sell t-shirts or laptop bags as well. But it can't have just any old look. The core of the brand must remain intact, as a marketing expert might put it.

This is how a record label is run successfully today, as a platform for releasing music, as a central point in networks of contacts, and as a generator of interest. Also as a project run by enthusiasts. But above all as one variable within a complex formula. The real money comes from elsewhere.

All labels operate like this, they just do so on different scales. Larger labels such as m_nus or Get Physical Records only diverge from this model in certain details. The dimensions of live gigs are larger and they have more control themselves. This is demonstrated by m_nus with its Contakt project, a massive tour of all the label's artists right across the world. Instead of having the artists booked to play in clubs, m_nus hires large concert venues and hosts the events itself. Or Get Physical, which is striving to market the duo Booka Shade throughout the world as its most prominent and successful live act. If things go according to plan, they may well succeed in crossing over to the pop market. If not, they can still try selling their music to television producers or licensing tracks for advertisements.

This kind of reshuffle is nothing new. When the music video appeared as a new medium in the mid-eighties it was regarded, in economic terms, as nothing other than a promotional tool to boost sales of the record. Now a similar change is taking place again. The tendency is for the music to function as a promotional clip to encourage people to attend concerts or DJ gigs. The same applies to both Dixon and Madonna. The fact that she's switched from her record label to a concert promoter doesn't mean that she won't be releasing any more music.

It's a development that Berkhahn the label boss regards with the composure of Dixon the DJ. 'The fact that playing live is gaining in importance is clearly good for us. We're good DJs; we can look forward to a rosy future – because I know that we'll get bookings. If people are spending less and less on musical media, but are hungry for music in a concert environment, then that works in our favour.'

Back to square one: Wednesday (reprise)

Wednesday is the day the records arrive. A few are already there by Tuesday, but most vinyl distributors deliver to the shops on a Wednesday. It's true that some DJs have switched to downloading their tunes as high-quality files from the internet and playing them off their laptop hard drives, which for them have replaced turntables. It's also the case, in Berlin in particular where so many producers live, that burned CDs are handed round with new, unreleased tracks. Nevertheless, the 12" vinyl record remains the leading format. The fact that the number of records in a pressing has fallen actually increases the pressure on DJs to go record shopping regularly. After all, when a record's gone, it's gone. If a record has been snapped up, it may not be too difficult to find it on the internet, but it can be relatively expensive, and it's certainly a pain. Besides, the need to stay up to date – which remains such a critical factor in house and techno – lies precisely in the fact that a record doesn't stay new for very long. Whilst the buzz lasts, that's when the record wants to be played. Which records a crowd will take to and which they won't – these are the questions that are resolved on the dance floor. Wednesdays are about preparation.

At Melting Point, for example, on Kastanienallee. It opened an hour earlier than usual today. Two new ultra-rare disco bootlegs have come in. The shop's owner made it known days ago that there would be five copies and five only; when they're sold out, they're sold out; there's no way to get any more in. Melting Point has five turntables where you can listen to the records for yourself, and they're all taken.

Melting Point is an institution. It was one of the first shops of any kind to open in the neighbourhood around Hackescher Markt, back when the area was still rather run down, long before tourist attractions such as the Hackesche Höfe were rebuilt and the gentrification of the area began. It has always specialised in house music, which didn't make for plain sailing in the Berlin of the nineties. After all, it was techno that set the tone here. When the rents in the area around Hackescher Markt became unaffordable the shop moved to Kastanienallee in Prenzlauer Berg. Now it stocks an equal measure of old and new records. Many of the secondhand collections have not even been sorted through yet; they're lying around in crates. And although there's a great deal of passing custom – Kastanienallee is one of the hotspots for trendy tourists – it survives, just like every other record shop, thanks to its loyal customer base, the DJs who come here week after week and are now standing at the turntables.

The same is true for Rotation Records, a couple of hundred metres down the road on Weinbergsweg, which focuses more on minimal house and techno. Here, too, the packages of records are just being opened and the DJs are scrambling for a place at the turntables. When Rotation opened in 2004 it was partially financed by The Circus hostel a couple of doors down. Rotation also has a solid customer base, including a few star DJs. Sometimes one of them will ring up because they're hung over or in a bad mood and ask for someone at the shop to put together a pile of the newest releases and send them over to their house in a taxi. Or someone will be stood at the counter on a Saturday afternoon who's come straight from an after-party and is in a rush to catch a plane to their next gig. They don't have time to go home, but they definitely need to pick up some records for their set, and they'll walk out with a whole bag full. These are the people that keep a shop going.

At Hardwax, the Kreuzberg institution beside the Landwehr canal, it's not quite so lively, but the assistant here is in a good mood too. Regardless of the vinyl crisis, when something really special gets released suddenly people start coming out of the woodwork.

Every record shop is a place of education, an institute for cultivating tastes. The manner of most record dealers brings to mind a cross between a small-time drug pusher and a university lecturer with little chance of becoming a professor. There are often moments when you're put in your place, but the authority of most record dealers is based on real enthusiasm and extensive knowledge. And sometimes, if the recipe is right, a record shop can also become a creative force itself. The techno and house genres, in particular, have seen many instances over the past twenty years where record shops have brought together a group of music aficionados in order to create something new. The most prominent example is probably Kompakt in Cologne. What was once founded as a branch of the Frankfurt shop Delirium is now a huge techno empire comprising various labels, an international distributor, a booking agency, a publisher and recording studios. And it's all housed in one building: the Factory of Cologne, the Bauhaus of minimal techno.

At Hardwax it's a similar set-up. Not only is it in alliance with Dubplates & Mastering, it's also surrounded by a collection of record labels founded on its fringes. The groundbreaking idea of the time – to cross techno with elements of dub – reflected the preferences of the guys running the shop, Mark Ernestus and Moritz von Oswald. They weren't particularly concerned about whether the rest of the world was interested, but then suddenly the rest of the world wanted Basic Channel records. It was a similar case in 2004, when Hardwax began to add to its repertoire a new style of music from London called dubstep. This genre is a culmination of grime, 2 step, drum'n'bass and dub. It typically features a stripped back sound, with plenty of space left between the drum beat and the killer bassline which drives the tracks. Here, too, the guys weren't particularly concerned about whether the Berliners wanted it – and they didn't, at first – they just trusted their own ears. Two years later, Ricardo Villalobos produced a high-profile mix of a dubstep track, thus firing the official starting shot for a process of cross-pollination between minimal techno and dubstep. In 2008, Hardwax was even able to shift two hundred copies of a new dubstep 12" within two weeks – there aren't many shops in London where these records sell better.

When Hardwax opened at the start of the nineties it was one of the very first German shops to sell this new music called techno. DJ Rok, who was a Tresor resident at the time, was the purchaser, feared for his unchallengeable appraisals. Killer or filler? That was his question. If it was just a filler, it didn't go on sale and was often thrown ostentatiously into the rubbish bin. DJ Hell and Electric Indigo also worked at Hardwax back then. It was sometimes a fearsome place, but it was also a great learning environment for the majority of Berlin and Brandenburg DJs.

These times are long gone. Hardwax is located at the centre of the techno universe, everyone knows it, and no one has anything to prove to anyone. It's a shop which is a pleasure to visit. In recent years a new generation of DJs, producers and label managers has congregated on its fringes. You might call the common thread which binds them together 'techno for techno lovers', although their musical output varies widely. Regardless of all the differences in sound, however, the house and techno blueprints of Mojuba, a.r.t.less, Millions of Moments or Styrax Leaves; the records on the artist-owned labels Cassy (Catherine Britton), MDR (Marcel Dettmann) or Soloaction (Shed) and the sine wave techno of Sleeparchive do exhibit a shared love for a certain roughness both in terms of sound and design. You could also call it purism: most of the records are enclosed in a paper sleeve, and the label is often simply stamped on the vinyl. However, you could also call it good business sense, as the records exude an exclusive, underground aura, whereas in fact the pressings are often just as large as those made by regular labels to release their tracks. It's just that they've saved on the artwork and aren't registered with the music author's society GEMA. It's rare for a record to get a second pressing, so if you want a limited, numbered copy from the first pressing on coloured vinyl, you'd better make regular visits to the shop.

Just like book shops and video rental shops, record shops are places where the transactions involve much more than simply passing goods over the sales counter. Here it's about knowledge – and often about hierarchies, as every shop holds onto certain records for its regular customers. It's also a matter of giving order to a tiny subdivision of the world. For instance, the 'Hardwax system' (as it's known, half jokingly, half respectfully, by all those who follow it) carries about the same weight as the national categorisation guidelines for public libraries, except here it's about separating records and musical styles. Its first tier of categorisation is geographical: Germany, Europe, England, USA, and the second tier is sorted by labels in alphabetical order. Sometimes a record shop is reminiscent of a Platonic Academy – the comparison is aided, of course, by the fact that they are populated almost entirely by men. Having said that, at Hardwax, despite its reputation as the pinnacle of the boys' techno world, there are more female staff than in any other record shop I know.

The next stop after Hardwax is Club der Visionäre, located by the water at the far end of Schlesische Straße, where Kreuzberg meets Treptow. Club der Visionäre is known for its after-parties. Now it's a Wednesday afternoon and people are sitting round drinking coffee and apple spritzers. A DJ has been on since midday; the music is plinking and plonking along nicely. You can't help looking around, out of curiosity, to see if anyone looks like they've been out partying since the weekend. But there's no one here who looks like they're reaching the end. This is where the week is getting started.

Indeed, Wednesday is the day that it all starts again.

It's an incredible summer, the summer of 2008 – no matter where you go, the promoters are wondering where all the people have come from. Later that night in Watergate is no exception – it's absolutely rammed, and on a Wednesday! The night is called 'The Odd Couple' and it's organised by the DJs Cle and Mike Vamp, two veterans of the Berlin club scene, also known as Martini Brös, who've been around since the early nineties. The upper dance floor is closed; the Waterfloor and the terrace on the Spree are open.

Who knows who all these people are. Snippets of Spanish, Italian, English and Swedish conversations flit back and forth. Very few come across as typical tourists though. Sometimes Rome and Stockholm, London and Seville are simply suburbs of Berlin. And whatever happens with the low-cost airlines, whether or not they survive the cut-throat competition with one another and the higher kerosene prices – if just a few of these countless guests remain in Berlin, it's a very positive result. No one wants a return to the bleak village-like Berlin of the eighties, nor a comeback of the nineties adventure playground for indigenous ravers. Other cities have a financial industry, large corporations, movie studios, fashion. Berlin has the German government, fine art and techno.

This night's going on to nine in the morning; I certainly won't be staying that long.

In the end I'm standing on the dance floor; around me are some Spanish girls and a few British guys; next to the DJ booth a small group of people are laughing and talking and Mike Vamp is playing a classic house track. The hour I originally planned to go home has long gone; out of the window the sky is growing brighter and beginning to light up with a pink-beige glow in the east; the calm surface of the Spree is more reminiscent of a lake than a river; a few dozen people are sitting out on the water terrace talking. I think to myself: life is good.

Twenty records: a brief history of the Berlin sound of the noughties

Ricardo Villalobos: Alcachofa
(Playhouse, 2003)

When it rains, it pours. Ricardo Villalobos spent over two years working on his album **Alcachofa**, and just at the point when the tracks were finished and he began playing them, the Berlin scene exploded. 'Dexter' and 'Easy Lee', the two big tracks from the album, became signature tunes of a new Berlin sound. Richie Hawtin had just moved here, as had Luciano, and the Perlon label had switched from Frankfurt to Berlin. Some parties lasted for days, moving from clubs into apartments and back to clubs again. And as people collectively scaled these heights and negotiated these lows, friendships were formed and careers gained a direction. **Alcachofa** relates all of this. This is not music for the peak time; this is music for the hours which follow, hours full of happiness, melancholy, joy, twistedness and the kind of overindulgence which can lead you on a slippery downward slope. There aren't many albums in electronic music which really deliver what the format demands – a personal signature, endurance, dramatic orchestration, artistic statement – in short, the ability to create a 'work'. This is one of those albums. It made Ricardo Villalobos into the biggest DJ star of the noughties.

Luciano: 'Orange Mistake'
(Cadenza, 2003)

For a while in Berlin you could be forgiven for having the feeling that the Chileans had taken over the city's night life. It wasn't just Ricardo Villalobos – a whole dozen Chileans were cavorting around the city, and their central figure was Luciano, who had previously lived in Switzerland. Like Villalobos, he brought a feeling for Latin-American rhythms, yet kept the music within the broad house mould. This Latin feeling comes from the percussion, although the end result sounds different to real Latin house. The jazzy rhythms which underpin his later records can already be detected here, but 'Orange Mistake' is driven by something else: time and again, above the clicking and whirring which supports the rhythm, the same rave signal can be heard sounding its message. A simple yet polished beat, overlaid with a killer sound which makes the music: it's a system which would go on to make the careers of several other producers.

Sleeparchive: 'Elephant Island'
(Sleeparchive, 2004)

It's impossible to overestimate the importance of the record shop Hardwax for the Berlin house and techno scene. As an institution for cultivating tastes, and as the promoter of a certain Berlin techno ethos, Hardwax insists that less is more. Less prominence, less superstar posturing, but also fewer sounds. At first, hardly anyone knew who was behind the Sleeparchive project. There was no name, there were no interviews, and when the secret was finally exposed and a certain Stephan Metzger made himself known, little else was known about the producer other than his name. These pieces have no story, but they have a sound: the sound of the raw, artistically unrefined bleeps and clonks of old synthesisers which many years ago were believed to hold the key to a technologically advanced future. It was around the mid-sixties, when the short-wave beeps of a home-made radio sounded as if they were the first step on the way to the moon landing. Retrofuturism is what we call it today – music which sounds like the seductive promises of a world we should have been living in long ago.

Nathan Fake: 'The Sky Was Pink', Holden remix (Border Community, 2004)

It's hard to imagine now how groundbreaking this record sounded at the time, what intense feelings it could trigger. The influence that 'The Sky Was Pink' had on techno music was demonstrated by the incredible speed at which the track's sounds were amalgamated into the universal techno vocabulary. Nathan Fake and his pal James Holden brought trance back to the dance floors of Berlin clubs, a genre which had been collectively shunned for several years. And this was trance in all its glory: big melodies, a structure which continuously builds towards the great climax, the moment when the synthesisers paint the sky pink (another Holden track is called 'A Break In The Clouds'). However, this was trance which had been rolling in the mud and which took its sound palette from various different genres. Some clear electronica influences shone through, a love for the wide-screen sounds of early-nineties guitar bands, and even minimal techno had left its trace. Of course, all of this would have been in vain if this sonic narrative of the night turning into light hadn't been so compelling. After several years of fragmentation, electronic dance music was searching for common ground once again.

John Tejada: 'Sweat On The Walls'
(Poker Flat, 2004)

It was an interesting paradox: while hipsters all over the world were identifying Berlin with a sound called electroclash, this mixture of electro beats and cocaine-champagne-Las-Vegas vocals never reached the dominant status that people assumed it had in places like Brooklyn, which ran parties under the name 'Berliniamsburg' in 2002. However, electroclash paved the way for a whole other sound which was then played all over Berlin: electro house. In 'Sweat On The Walls' by the Californian producer John Tejada you can hear how electroclash collapses and makes way for something else. The vocals – a sexy female voice tinged with Sunday-afternoon boredom talking about a party where sweat had been dripping from the walls – are still part of the old format, but the music has moved on. It's a fresh, forceful house track with a smattering of acid.

Booka Shade: 'Mandarine Girl'
(Get Physical, 2005)

The other major success story among Berlin labels in the noughties, alongside Richie Hawtin's m_nus, belongs to Get Physical. Five veterans of the Frankfurt scene wanted to make another go of things in 2002 and moved to the capital. They were DJ T., alias Thomas Koch, former editor of **Groove** magazine, Patrick Bodmer and Philipp Jung, who together form the DJ duo M.A.N.D.Y., and Walter Merziger and Arno Kammermeier, alias Booka Shade, who had already made it as very successful techno producers in the nineties. The latter are the musical brains of the label. They were behind almost all the productions in its early stages, and in 'Mandarine Girl' and 'Body Language' they came up with two archetypal electro house tracks. One is trance-tinged house music for moments of dance floor emotion, the other is an up-tempo shuffle bathed in shimmering light. Both hit sales in the tens of thousands, enormous figures for vinyl records. Since then Booka Shade have been touring the big arenas of the world with an elaborate live show. They're one of the few Berlin house acts who've managed to cross over to an audience outside of the clubbing scene.

Âme: 'Rej'
(Innervisions, 2005)

It's a nice feeling when musical boundaries come tumbling down. With 'Rej', the borders between house, electro and techno became so porous that it was no longer possible to say for sure if the track was beating with the pulse of one type of dance floor or another. This was a record that absolutely every DJ had in their box, one which they could 'all agree on', as you tend to say of such hits. The guys behind Âme are Frank Wiedemann and Kristian Beyer, two producers from Karlsruhe who had, up to that point, been musically at home at the deeper end of house music. For their first record on the Berlin label Innervisions they supercharged a powerful tech-house groove with a beeping Morse tone which evolves into a melody. It's a classic track, purged of all unnecessary frills, perfect down to the last detail.

Troy Pierce: 'Horse Nation'
(m_nus, 2005)

Suddenly the term was on everyone's lips: ketamine house. It's not as if the release of tracks like 'Horse Nation' suddenly caused herds of people to fill their nostrils with ketamine – a strong horse tranquiliser which leads, upon consumption, to a feeling of falling down a deep 'K-hole', an experience which has both its frightening and its fascinating moments. Ketamine had always been around as a coming-down drug for the quieter, post-euphoric hours, and it wasn't taken any more or less in 2005 than the years before or since. Ketamine house, however, was a fitting and vivid description for a bleak, minimalist house sound which had been thoroughly cooled at its core. 'Horse Nation' is a track driven by irritations: voices which flit through the room, drum rolls you can't quite localise, noises which sound like virtual convicts dragging virtual balls and chains over real prison yards. This is incredibly radical music – incredible when you consider that m_nus boss Richie Hawtin has managed, since moving over to Berlin, to make himself and his label's artists into one of the machines driving the success of this music.

Theo Parrish: 'Falling Up', Carl Craig remix
(Third Ear, 2006)

This track hit like a bomb, and not only because it involved a collaboration between two of the most renowned Detroit producers, Carl Craig and Theo Parrish. Limited to a few hundred copies, it sold out within a few days and was played all over the place from that point on. With his remix of 'Falling Up', Carl Craig excels more than ever in his very own art of standing with one foot in the blackest funk, the other in the whitest synth pop, and turning this tension into great drama. What starts with the harmless house groove of a simple kick drum and a Fender Rhodes piano then transforms into a dark, peak-time bass monster. It was the first in a long line of brilliant Carl Craig remixes in the last few years. Almost all were exceptional, but none better than this.

Rhythm & Sound: 'Free For All', Soundstream remix
(Burial Mix, 2006)

German techno and house productions are not so hot on vocals. Neither the tradition of the diva singer nor that of the preacher have deep roots in this country. We'd sooner stick a voice through a vocoder first so it sounds like a man-machine. As such, the ten reggae singers who recorded the vocals for Rhythm & Sound are like a godsend. This was a project by the Basic Channel founders Mark Ernestus and Moritz von Oswald which evolved over the years from dub techno into roots reggae. The remixes of the tracks couldn't be more different, but surely the most beautiful comes from Soundstream, who otherwise specialises in cut-up disco. He transforms the original, featuring vocals from Paul St. Hilaire, into a scintillating deep house track. A classic.

Samim & Michal: 'Exercize'
(Freizeitglauben, 2007)

If there's one genre that Berlin was identified with all over the world in the mid-noughties, it was 'minimal'. Ultra-stripped-back, bone dry house. Samim & Michal's 'Exercize' is textbook minimal. The track chimes and chirps like a toy clock, rattles as if it has some screws loose, but it never becomes overloaded; it always leaves room to spare. The driving element here is the snare, not the kick drum, and over all this you can hear the wandering reverberations of an otherworldly voice. Classic after-party music for Sunday afternoon dance floors. Records like these can't be blamed for the fact that a backlash set in shortly afterwards, that minimal became a dirty word and hipsters started walking down Kastanienallee wearing anti-minimal T-shirts. The formula was just so simple and seductive that ultimately every Tom, Dick and Harry had a go at recording and releasing their own minimal track.

Dettmann/Klock: 'Dawning/Dead Man Watches The Clock'
(Ostgut Tonträger, 2006)

Every track in a DJ set is defined not only by the tracks which precede and follow it, but also by the sound system through which you hear the music. The whole techno blueprint that Marcel Dettmann and Ben Klock have developed is inextricably linked with the system, the dance floor and the crowd of Berghain. The pair are both resident DJs there, and this is where they began slightly reducing the tempo of their epic DJ sets, yet without diminishing the potent force of the music. This is majestic techno, stripped back and raw, slow and clear. Music which knows what minimal is, but has thrown all superfluous clicks and clacks overboard. For a long time, you may have had the feeling that the various genres of dance music were moving closer together. On the vast Berghain dance floor, however, techno's true spirit suddenly began to sound like the most exciting music in the world once more.

Ricardo Villalobos: 'Fizheuer Zieheuer'
(Playhouse, 2006)

The rumours started circulating before the track did. Ricardo's new record is 37 minutes long, people were telling each other long before the release of 'Fizheuer Zieheuer', and the respect for this radical gesture audible in the tone of almost everyone talking about it was clearly mixed with scepticism. Can something like that work? What's the loon going to come up with next? The track is in fact an epic remix of 'Pobjednicki Cocek', a piece by the Romanian wind orchestra Blehorkestar Bakija Bakic. Villalobos samples a couple of brass sections, endlessly loops the samples, puts them through a dub-effect mill, and after what feels like an eternity, releases them in a grand crescendo. Then it carries on. Anyone who heard this for the first time on a dance floor without knowing what kind of track it was, ideally in one of Villalobos' own sets, undoubtedly experienced one of those moments which you never forget because, for a short time, you feel like you're on a hotline to the heavens.

Efdemin: 'Just A Track'
(Dial, 2007)

Along with Larry Heard's wonderful 'The Sun Can't Compare', Efdemin's 'Just A Track' pointed in a direction which was to lead many Berlin DJs and producers out of their minimal cul-de-sac: the direction was deepness. Hardly anyone immediately went away and imitated entire deep house tracks, however. Instead, they took a single element – in 'Just A Track' this was the voice of the preacher who explains who would become president if house were a nation (he himself, obviously) – and combined this with what was otherwise still an extremely minimalist track. Others took a syncopated electric piano sound. This didn't change the framework a great deal, but, to cut the story short, where psychedelic had been before, spirituality was now in its place. It's not such a giant leap, after all.

Mari Boine: 'Vuoi Vuoi Me' Henrik Schwarz remix
(Universal Jazz, 2007)

Somewhat outside the main genres, but highly rated from all sides, Henrik Schwarz has spent several years tinkering with his very own blueprint for a kind of house music which is rooted in soul, funk and jazz, but does more than merely sample past greats or indulge in nostalgia. Schwarz produces, plays with other jazz musicians and remixes other people's productions, and he does so with considerable success. Take his remix of Mari Boine, a Norwegian singer from Lapland whose style – a blend of yoik (a form of song from the indigenous peoples of northern Norway), jazz, folk and rock – is assigned, for want of a better alternative, to the huge category of world music. Schwarz lends 'Vuoi Vuoi Me' a timeless deep-house groove which he builds up to epic breadth with his liberal use of strings. The result is simply wonderful.

Matt John: 'Olga Dancekowski'
(Bar 25, 2007)

The longer the weekend goes on, the more the confusion builds. 'Olga Dancekowski' could be described as an archetypal afterparty track: the kick drum has been considerably reduced, as hardly anyone on the dance floor still wants to take a pounding from the music at this hour. The track's structure is not too far removed from that of a classic techno record, but the sound is quite different. Matt John uses bleeps, bloops and toots which sound like they could be coming from a doll's house which has come to life at night. He once called his style 'holographic music', and if this is meant in the sense that the music always allows for multiple perspectives, it's a fitting term. Various elements can act as your guide through the track; it depends entirely on which sound you mentally latch onto. In any case, 'Olga Dancekowski' takes you on quite a trip. It's psychedelic computer music which is both profound and silly, and as vibrant as the multi-coloured building blocks of the Ableton interface.

Radio Slave: 'No Sleep Part 4'
(Rekids, 2008)

Producers are all complaining about the decline in sales and saying it's no longer financially viable to make music. If you look at the excessive output of Matt Edwards, alias Radio Slave, you might assume that he's drawn a simple conclusion from this dilemma: if records are only selling half as well, you have to release twice as many! He came to Berlin in 2006, and since that time hardly a week has gone by without a track, a remix or an edit of his being released, or a new record coming out on his label Rekids. 'Grindhouse Tool' is precisely what the title implies, a mean tech house monster; 'Tantakatan' is apparently based on a Herbie Hancock sample, but it actually sounds like classic Matt Edwards. You can recognise those drum arrangements from the next room; the way they march straight on with such force is unmistakable. These are bolts which will tighten the screws on any dance floor.

DJ Koze: 'I Want To Sleep'
(IRR, 2008)

DJ Koze is the surrealist amongst house producers. From day one he has been tinkering with his own idiosyncratic world of sound – ludicrous, colourful, and instilled with a different kind of logic. There's always one element or another which has gone off track, something out of sorts. Even when Koze makes such a wonderfully somnambulant track as 'I Want To Sleep', he has to put in a strange static noise which comes in every few bars as if to say, 'Attention! I am a DJ Koze track!' And as if that weren't disorienting enough, two thirds of the way through a female voice starts to explain in a far-flung language what she thinks about whilst she's doing her laundry. The name of the label is fitting: International Records Recordings – not everyone could have come up with that either. This is music for the most extraordinary hours. But then, there's really no shortage of those, is there?

Portable: 'Knowone Can Take Away'
(Perlon, 2008)

Without the input of certain labels, including Perlon, the Berlin sound of the noughties would have been quite different. Zip, Morane, Ricardo Villalobos, Thomas Melchior, without ever really forming a stylistic school, produced a group of records for Perlon which all share a certain attitude, even if this is simply an austerity in the way they go about making music. Although it wasn't always the case, this was often very abstract music. It's therefore all the more remarkable what the South African Alan Abrahams, alias Portable, produced for his track 'Release': a genuinely heart-rending house track where he sings – over melancholy synth lines and a house beat – about his wish to be released from the constraints of a relationship that is falling apart.

Almost all these tracks can be downloaded from online stores like Kompakt or Beatport. Of course, the most enjoyable way to buy music is in record shops, and some of these records can still be found there too. Aside from these tracks, the mix CDs of Berghain/Panoramabar or Watergate are to be recommended as an introduction to the Berlin sound of recent years. Also well worth a listen are the mix CD series 'Boogy Bytes' on Bpitch Control and 'Body Language' on Get Physical Records.

Thanks

Many thanks to Andreas Becker, Steffen Berkhahn, Kristian Beyer, Heike Blümner, Matthias Bohmbach, Achim Brandenburg, Catherine Britton, Mark Butler, Maja Classen, Pauline Drewfs, Laura Ewert, Christine Giese, Martin Gorges, Steffen Hack, Dimitri Hegemann, Robert Henke, Nick Höppner, Joanna Itzek, Carsten Joost, Christoph Klenzendorf, Stephan Krasser, Olaf Kretschmar, Tanja Mühlhans, Andrew Rasse, Georg Roske, Carolin Saage, Nikolaus Schäfer, Anja Schneider, Phillip Sollmann, Robert Stadler, Dave Turov, Ricardo Villalobos, Alexis Waltz, Julian Weber, Benjamin Weiss, Frank Wiedemann.

Without my copy editor Karsten Kredel I'd never have started or finished the German version of this book, and without the producer Nina Knapitsch it probably wouldn't have been published until the bulldozers had well and truly flattened Bar 25.

Thanks to Paul Sabin for his faithful translation, and to Nicholas Grindell for proof-reading it.

I'd also like to thank my family.

Sources

The chapter 'Ricardo' was published in a different form in **Spex**, issue 6/2007.

Part of the chapter 'Berghain, the centre of the world' by Alexis Waltz was published in **Groove**, issue 3/2008.

The chapter 'Rave mother, rave daughter' was published in **De:Bug**, issue 9/2007.